The Chartered
Institute of Marketing

CIM Companion:

international marketing strategy

CIM Publishing

CIM Publishing

The Chartered Institute of Marketing
Moor Hall
Cookham
Berkshire
SL6 9QH

www.cim.co.uk

First published 2002
© CIM Publishing 2002

Series Editors: Mark Stuart and John Ling.

Applications for the copyright holder's written permission to reproduce any part of this publication should be addressed to the Editors at the publisher's address.

It is the publisher's policy to use paper manufactured from sustainable forests.

British Library Cataloguing in Publication Data
A CIP catalogue record for this book can be obtained from the British Library.

ISBN 0 902130 89 7

Printed and bound by The Cromwell Press, Trowbridge, Wiltshire.
Cover design by Marie-Claire Bonhommet.

contents

Study guide

This Companion is written to complement the recommended core texts:

Doole & Lowe, 2001, *International Marketing Strategy*, 3rd Edition, Thomson Learning.

Paliwoda and Thomas, 1997, *International Marketing*, 3rd Edition, Butterworth-Heinemann.

Ambler & Styles, 2000, *The SILK Road to International Marketing*, Prentice-Hall.

Usunier, 2000, *Marketing Across Cultures*, 3rd Edition, Prentice-Hall.

International marketing strategy is a topic that involves knowledge of both marketing and business strategy so this Companion offers framework for study rather than a complete text.

It also aims to offer you support as either an individual or group learner as you move further along the road to becoming a competent and proficient marketer, recognising that change will always produce opportunities for new and experiential learning at every stage in your career.

The process of learning within this Companion has two important elements:

Understanding marketing concepts and their application

The study text in the following Sessions has been deliberately written to highlight the concepts that you will need to grasp as you start to understand international marketing fundamentals, what marketing can achieve, and how it is implemented. The material is described briefly and concisely, to enable you to cover a range of key material at this level. It does not attempt to be fully comprehensive, and you should read widely from other sources, including the recommended course text (readings are specified for each of the Sessions in this book, and shown in Table 2 which follows), the marketing press and national newspapers, to develop your understanding of the concepts introduced here. More comprehensive marketing textbooks are details on the module reading list, and provide a wider context for the concepts explained in this Companion, and provide more Case Studies and examples to illustrate marketing in practice. It is also expected that you will be familiar with the range of marketing journals and business press that are relevant to study at this level.

How to use this Companion

Each Session is devoted to a small section of the syllabus and is designed to provide a simple framework to help you 'get to grips' with the topic. At this level students are expected to read a wide range of appropriate texts and journals, but it is appreciated that time is possibly the scarcest resource. Therefore, where possible, activities and examples refer back to those that are in the recommended core texts for this module.

Each Session has a minimum of three activities with feedback to these give at the end of the relevant Session. At the end of each Session there are three projects which are designed to help the student find ways of further developing knowledge and understanding about the topic. No feedback is given for these but it will be advantageous to compare answers with fellow students and colleagues if appropriate.

It is recommended that you complete the reading for each Session to familiarise yourself with the topic before undertaking the activities in the text.

The Companion follows the order of the syllabus for this module and references for models and diagrams referred to, in the text, are listed Table 3.

Table 1 – Web sites

www.connectedinmarketing.com	
www.connectedinmarketing.com/cim/index.cfm	
www.cimvirtualinstitute.com	
www.marketingportal.cim.co.uk	Includes CIM Marketing Trends Surveys (MTS).
www.adslogans.co.uk	Online database of advertising slogans enabling marketers to check whether a slogan is already in use.
www.ipa.co.uk	Institute of Practitioners in Advertising.
www.asa.org.uk	Advertising Standards Agency.
www.new-marketing.org	Research updates into new marketing issues, customer segmentation and repercussions for marketing practitioners.
www.wapforum.org	Industry association responsible for creating the standards for WAP (Wireless Application Protocol).
www.prnewswire.co.uk	UK media monitoring service – reviews mentions in all media types (print, online publications and broadcast).
www.keynote.co.uk	Market research reports.
www.verdict.co.uk	Retail research reports.
www.datamonitor.com	Market analysis providing global data collection and in-depth analysis across any industry.
www.store.eiu.com	Economist Intelligence Unit providing country-specific global business analysis.
www.mintel.com	Consumer market research.
www.royalmail.co.uk	General marketing advice and information.
www.ft.com	Financial Times online newspaper and archives.
www.afxpress.com	Business news plus industry trends.
www.export.org.uk	Institute of Export.
www.worldmarketing.org	World Marketing Association.
www.statistics.gov.uk	Office for national statistics (UK).
www.homeoffice.gov.uk	Research development statistics.
www.business.com	Business search engine.
www.mad.co.uk	Marketing Week online.

www.bbc.co.uk/edu	News online, Learning Zone and much more.
www.thetimes.co.uk	Times newspaper online.
www.open.gov.uk	Gateway to a wide range of UK government information.
www.durlacher.com	Latest research on business use of the Internet.
www.cyberatlas.com	Regular updates on the latest Internet developments from a business perspective.
www.whatis.com	Directory of Internet terms.
www.ecommercetimes.com	Daily news on the latest e-business developments.
www.nikkeibp.asiabiztech.com	AsiaBizTech is a source of business and technology information focused upon Japan and Asia.
www.ecasa.org.za	The Electronic Commerce Association of South Africa promotes the use of electronic commerce to improve commercial, industrial and government business efficiency.
www.worldmarketing.org	World Marketing Association promotes best practice and exchange of information among marketing associations from around the world.
www.asiasource.org	Provides information on events across Asia.
www.ec-europe.org	Electronic Commerce Europe co-ordinates and assists the development of electronic commerce in Europe.
www.ansi.org	American National Standards Institute – represents US business interests with respect to the Internet.
www.ama.org	American Marketing Association.
wwwkpmg.co.uk www.eyuk.com www.anderson.com www.pwcglobal.com	Major consultancy company web sites with research reports.
www.emerald-library.com	Full text journal articles on a range of business topics – practical and theoretical.
www.hbsp.harvard.edu	Free abstracts from Harvard Business Review articles.
www.mckinseyquarterly.com	Free full texts articles on globalisation, economic development and cultural issues.
www.oecd.org	Organisation for Economic Co-operation and Development.
www.eiu.com	Economic Intelligence Unit.
www.globalexchange.org	Global Exchange is dedicated to promoting ties around the world.

The following table identifies web sites that you will find are particularly useful for specific Sessions:

Session	Web sites
Session 1	www.thomsonlearning.co.uk/internationalmarketing www.ita.doc.gov/ www.census.gov/foreign-trade
Session 2	www.wto.org www.globalexchange.org www.ita.doc.gov/tradestats www.worldbank.com
Session 3	www.eiu.com www.ciafactbook.com
Session 4	www.unilever.com www.pg.com www.dataweb.usitc.gov/
Session 5	www.infoexport.gc.ac www.tradepartners.gov.uk www.dti.gov.uk/export.control.uk www.devicelink.com
Session 6	www.mmc.com
Session 7	www.britishchambers.org.uk www.ce.cei.gov.cn
Session 8	www.anheuser-busch.com www.gbrands.com www.accenture.com
Session 9	www.unilever.com www.ciafactbook.com
Session 10	www.intracen.org/ www.businessweek.com www.brandchannel.com
Session 11	www://pacific.commerce.ubc.ca/xr/currency_table.html
Session 12	www.finfacts.ie/brands2001 www.globadstrategies.com www.global-advertising.com www.adageglobal.com www.mrmworldwide.com

Session	Web sites
Session 13	www.relationshipmktg.com www.fita.org/ www.aarm.org www.allen.com
Session 14	www.shipment.com www.globaldistribution.com uk.cambridge.org/information/introduction/distribution.htm www.amadeus.net
Session 15	www.census.gov/ftp/pub/foreign-trade

Table 2 – Background reading

The following references are suggested background readings for each Session. It is suggested that the student undertake this reading before studying the relevant Companion Session.

Session	Reading from core text: Doole & Lowe, 2001, International Marketing Strategy, 3rd Edition, Thomson Learning. Paliwoda and Thomas, 1997, International Marketing, 3rd Edition, Butterworth-Heinemann. Ambler & Styles, 2000, The SILK Road to International Marketing, Prentice-Hall. Usunier, 2000, Marketing Across Cultures, 3rd Edition, Prentice-Hall.
Session 1	**Doole & Lowe, International Marketing Strategy** Chapter 1: An Introduction to International Marketing **Paliwoda and Thomas, International Marketing** Chapter 1: Internationalisation: a necessity not a luxury but does corporate behaviour reflect it? **Ambler & Styles, The SILK Road to International Marketing** Chapter 1: One Touch of Nature
Session 2	**Doole & Lowe, International Marketing Strategy** Chapter 2: The International Trading Environment **Usunier, Marketing Across Cultures** Chapter 6: The Convergence of marketing Environments Worldwide
Session 3	**Paliwoda and Thomas, International Marketing** Chapter 2: Environmental Marketing: the 'SLEPT' and 'C' factors **Usunier, Marketing Across Cultures** Chapter 6: The Convergence of marketing Environments Worldwide
Session 4	**Doole & Lowe, International Marketing Strategy** Chapter 3: Social and Cultural considerations in International Marketing **Usunier, Marketing Across Cultures** Chapter 2: Cultural Dynamics: Time and space Chapter 3: Cultural Dymanics: Interactions, mindsets and behaviours

Session 5	**Doole & Lowe, International Marketing Strategy** Chapter 4: International Marketing Research and opportunity Analysis **Ambler & Styles, The SILK Road to International Marketing** Chapter 4: How Marketing Decisions are Made **Usunier, Marketing Across Cultures** Chapter 7: Cross-cultural Market Research
Session 6	**Doole & Lowe, International Marketing Strategy** Chapter 5: International Marketing Planning and Organisation **Paliwoda and Thomas, International Marketing** Chapter 9: International Marketing Planning; Reviewing, appraising and implementing **Ambler & Styles, The SILK Road to International Marketing** Chapter 5: Organisational Learning: International planning process Chapter 6: Passion: Creating commitment, purpose and identity
Session 7	**Ambler & Styles, The SILK Road to International Marketing** Chapter 3: What International Managers Do
Session 8	**Doole & Lowe, International Marketing Strategy** Chapter 7: Globalisation **Ambler & Styles, The SILK Road to International Marketing** Chapter 8: Not invented here: Internationalising innovation **Usunier, Marketing Across Cultures** Chapter 5: Local Consumers and the Globalisation of Consumers Chapter 8: Intercultural Marketing Strategy
Session 9	**Doole & Lowe, International Marketing Strategy** Chapter 8: Market Entry Strategies **Paliwoda and Thomas, International Marketing** Chapter 4: Market Entry Modes: strategic considerations of direct versus indirect involvement **Ambler & Styles, The SILK Road to International Marketing** Chapter 9: "Does this apply to me?" Adjusting for sectors
Session 10	**Doole & Lowe, International Marketing Strategy** Chapter 9: International Product Management **Paliwoda and Thomas, International Marketing** Chapter 5: International Product Policy Considerations **Usunier, Marketing Across Cultures** Chapter 9: Product Policy: Physical, service and symbolic attributes Chapter 10: Product Policy: Managing meaning

Session 11	**Doole & Lowe, International Marketing Strategy** Chapter 12: Pricing for International Markets **Paliwoda and Thomas, International Marketing** Chapter 6: Pricing, Credit and Terms of doing Business **Usunier, Marketing Across Cultures** Chapter 11: The Critical Role of Price in Relational Exchange
Session 12	**Doole & Lowe, International Marketing Strategy** Chapter 10: International Communications and Internet Marketing **Paliwoda and Thomas, International Marketing** Chapter 8: Promotion within the Foreign Market **Ambler & Styles, The SILK Road to International Marketing** Chapter 10: Digital Relationships Chapter 11: Connectivity for the Global marketer **Usunier, Marketing Across Cultures** Chapter 13: Language, Culture and Communications Chapter 14:Advertising Chapter 15: Personal Selling, Networking and Public Relations
Session 13	**Usunier, Marketing Across Cultures** Chapter 16: People, trust and Tasks
Session 14	**Doole & Lowe, International Marketing Strategy** Chapter 11: The Management of International Distribution and Logistics **Paliwoda and Thomas, International Marketing** Chapter 7: Strategic International Logistical and Distribution Decisions **Ambler & Styles, The SILK Road to International Marketing** Chapter 2: Relationships for the Long haul **Usunier, Marketing Across Cultures** Chapter 12: International Distribution and Sales promotion
Session 15	**Ambler & Styles, The SILK Road to International Marketing** Chapter 7: International Marketing Metrics

Table 3 – Marketing models

The text in the Companion Sessions refer to appropriate models but does not reproduce these as they can be seen in the core textbooks. The references for these are supplied in the following table. Please note that this does not necessarily represent the full range of models that you will need to study for your exam or assessment.

Session	Marketing model	Reference:
Session 1	■ Environmental influences on international marketing.	Doole & Lowe p10
	■ 'Big Mac index'.	Doole & Lowe p16
Session 2	■ Regional composition of world GDP and population.	Doole & Lowe p33
	■ Tariff and non-tariff barriers.	Doole & Lowe p40
Session 3	■ Country associated risks.	Doole & Lowe p22
Session 4	■ A cultural framework.	Doole & Lowe p66
	■ Cultural influences on buyer behaviour.	Doole & Lowe p72
	■ Model of consumer behaviour in international markets.	Doole & Lowe p76
	■ Contextual continuum of differing cultures (Hall).	Doole & Lowe p80
	■ Power distance/individualism dimensions across cultures.	Doole & Lowe p82
	■ Interrelationship between context and diffusion.	Doole & Lowe p84
Session 5	■ Product/market combinations and scope for competitive advantage on market entry (Gilligan & Hird 1985).	Doole & Lowe p97
	■ Four risk matrix.	Doole & Lowe p100
	■ Business portfolio matrix (Harrell & Kiefer 1993).	Doole & Lowe p102
	■ 12C framework.	Doole & Lowe p107

Session	Marketing model	Reference:
	■ Market profile analysis framework.	Doole & Lowe p108
	■ Online databases (examples).	Doole & Lowe p111
	■ Perceptions about quality and accessibility of information in the Asia-Pacific region.	Doole & Lowe p113
	■ International market research process.	Doole & Lowe p115
Session 6	■ International marketing strategy process.	Doole & Lowe p29
	■ Stakeholder demands on the firm.	Doole & Lowe p156
	■ Ansoff growth matrix.	Doole & Lowe p159
	■ McKinsey 7S Framework.	Doole & Lowe p161
Session 7	■ Examples of organisational structures.	Doole & Lowe p168, p170
Session 8	■ Examples of transnational companies.	Doole & Lowe p215
	■ Alternative worldwide strategies.	Doole & Lowe p225
	■ Globalisation push and pull factors.	Doole & Lowe p227
	■ Global 1-to-1 marketing.	Doole & Lowe p237
	■ Unseen dangers in foreign investment.	Doole & Lowe p239
Session 9	■ Market entry methods and levels of involvement in international markets.	Doole & Lowe p248
	■ Risk and control in market entry.	Doole & Lowe p249
	■ Initiation and development of export product portfolios.	Doole & Lowe p257
Session 10	■ Elements of products and services.	Doole & Lowe p295

Session	Marketing model	Reference:
	■ International product life cycle.	Doole & Lowe p307
	■ BCG matrix.	Doole & Lowe p309
	■ Brand value equation.	Doole & Lowe p314
	■ Brand valuation.	Doole & Lowe p315
	■ International branding model.	Doole & Lowe p317
	■ New product categories.	Doole & Lowe p320
	■ For and against centralised R&D.	Doole & Lowe p324
Session 11	■ Three types of grey market.	Doole & Lowe p426
	■ Framework for selecting a co-ordination method.	Doole & Lowe p428
	■ The export order process.	Doole & Lowe p438
Session 12	■ External, internal and interactive marketing.	Doole & Lowe p330
	■ Dimensions of external marketing.	Doole & Lowe p331
	■ Push and pull strategies.	Doole & Lowe p341
	■ Internal and external communications.	Doole & Lowe p344
Session 13	■ Dimensions of transaction and relationship marketing.	Doole & Lowe p363
	■ Traditional relationship marketing.	Doole & Lowe p364
	■ Partnership linkages.	Doole & Lowe p364
	■ The 'six' markets.	Doole & Lowe p366
Session 14	■ Distribution channels for business and consumer goods.	Doole & Lowe p375
	■ Differences between retailers in developed and developing countries.	Doole & Lowe p386
	■ Export order and physical distribution process.	Doole & Lowe p402
Session 15	No additional models.	

Session 1

International marketing

Introduction

This first Session forms an introduction to international marketing and begins by considering the development and extent of international trading. It explores how the different markets can be categorised and outlines some of the significant challenges faced by international traders including marketing strategy, quality and service issues and ethical dilemmas.

LEARNING OUTCOMES

At the end of this Session you will be able to:

- Explain different types of markets in the international trading environment.

- Discuss the strategic and contextual elements of global operations – global and multinational marketing as strategic choices.

- Discuss international networks and supply chains.

- Explain the consequences of a more ethical, responsible approach to global corporate operations.

Development of international trade

International trade is a vital part of world economic activity but it is not a new phenomenon. Whilst the growth of international trade has accelerated in the last forty years, it goes back far beyond then and has been developing throughout the ages since the time when barter was used. The great growth period for trade was in the eighteenth and nineteenth centuries when many of today's important trading links were forged and developed. As we will see in Session 2, when world trading patterns are studied in some depth, international trade in merchandise now exceeds US $7 trillion in a global marketplace consisting of a population of 10 billion people. Whilst most of us cannot visualise such huge amounts, it does serve to give some indication of the scale of international trade today and the opportunities in international marketing. The reading for this Session from *International Marketing Strategy* (Doole & Lowe) examines a number of these opportunities and looks at the importance of international marketing in today's international trading environment.

Theory of comparative advantage

The rationale for world trade is based largely upon the Theory of Comparative Advantage developed by the classical economist David Ricardo. At its simplest level, the theory suggests that trade between countries takes place because one country is able to produce a product at a lower price than is possible elsewhere.

Porter (1990) suggests that countries can build a national advantage through four major attributes:

- **Factor conditions:** the nation's position in factors of production such as skilled labour or infrastructure necessary to compete.
- **Demand conditions:** the nature of demand in the home country.
- **Related and supporting industries:** the presence or absence of supplier industries and related industries that are internationally competitive.
- **Firm strategy, structure and rivalry:** the conditions in the nation governing how companies are created, organised and managed and the nature of domestic rivalry.

The theory of comparative advantage is often used as the classic explanation of world trade. Other observers, however, believe that world trade and investment patterns are based upon the product life cycle concept and that, at an international level, products move through four distinct phases:

1. Manufacture for the home market and the start of exporting.
2. Foreign production starts.
3. Foreign products become increasingly competitive in world markets.
4. Imports to the home country begin providing significant competition.

Although the product life cycle provides an interesting insight into the evolution of multinational operations, it needs to be recognised that it provides only a partial explanation of world trade since products do not inevitably follow this pattern.

Firstly, competition today is international rather than domestic for all goods and services. Consequently, there is a reduced time lag between product research, development and production, leading to the simultaneous appearance of a standardised product in major world markets. Secondly, it is not production in the highly labour-intensive industries which is moving to the low labour cost countries but the capital intensive industries such as electronics, creating the anomalous situation of basing production for high value, high technology goods in the countries least able to afford them. Nor does the model go very far in explaining the rapid development of companies networking production and marketing facilities across many countries. Thus global business integration and sharing of R&D, technological and business resources is seen as a more relevant explanation of today's world trade.

It is estimated that somewhere in the region of 70% of international trade is now by global or multi-domestic corporations trading with each other. More and more industrial products sold throughout the world are assembled in one country from components manufactured in others. Thus world trade is becoming more inter-dependent and the pattern of world trading becoming in many ways more complex to understand, as firms seek to gain a competitive advantage amongst the vast range of countries across the globe. It is the opportunities and challenges that this presents that are studied in the next section.

Activity 1.1

Scan the business sections of the international trade press over a period of a week. Make a note of the companies in the news and the competitive challenges they are facing in their global markets.

Challenge of international marketing

Amongst the 200 or so countries in the world, there are varying economic conditions, levels of economic development and GNP per capita. This gives rise to a number of differing market structures across the world. In studying international marketing it is important to have an understanding of the opportunities and challenges such different structures present and how they impinge on a marketing strategy.

One of the key challenges facing companies trying to develop an integrated strategy across a number of international markets is the divergent levels of economic development they have to deal with, making it often very difficult to have a cohesive strategy, certainly in pricing. The Big Mac index in Chapter 1 of Doole & Lowe is a measure of how long a worker has to work to earn enough to buy a Big Mac. It shows that the average worker in Caracas has to work for 117 minutes to earn enough money to buy a Big Mac, while at the other extreme, a worker in Tokyo needs to work for only nine minutes.

It is usual to categorise this vast array of markets into three types of economies:

- **The developed economies:** The economies of the USA/Canada, European Union and Japan account for 80% of world trade. For many firms this constitutes much of what is termed the global market. It is from this triangle that the global consumer with similar lifestyles, needs and desires emanates.

- **The emerging economies:** These include countries such as China, Brazil, Vietnam and India where there is a huge and growing demand for everything from cars to cellular phones. Many of the countries which were seen only a few years ago as 'Less Developed Countries' (LDCs) show a healthy economic advancement and now fall under the umbrella of emerging markets. Countries such as Indonesia, China, Mexico, Brazil, Chile, Hungary, Poland, Turkey, the Czech Republic and South Africa are all viewed as key growth markets. Emerging markets are now becoming more economically powerful and moving up the ranks such that by the year 2020 it is projected that China, South Korea and Taiwan will be amongst the top tier of national economies.

- **Less Developed Countries (LDCs):** This group includes underdeveloped countries and developing countries. The main features are a low GDP per capita, a limited amount of manufacturing activity and a very poor and fragmented infrastructure. Typical infrastructure weaknesses are in transport, communications, education and health care. In addition, the public sector is often viewed as slow-moving, bureaucratic and sometimes corrupt. Whilst such markets may potentially be attractive to companies as long-term opportunities, the bureaucracy is seen by many as being a crippling trade barrier.

It is common to find that LDCs are heavily reliant on one product and often on one trading partner. In many LDCs this product is the main export earner. Three quarters of LDCs depend on their main trading partner for more than one quarter of their export revenue. The risks posed to the LDC by changing patterns of supply and demand are great; falling commodity prices can result in large decreases in earnings for the whole country.

Activity 1.2

Scan the quality press used for Activity 1.1.

For each of the different types of markets identified, find news stories in a particular country which will impact on the competitive activity of international firms competing in those markets.

Consider how the challenges vary between the different types of market.

What is an international market?

International marketing can be defined as existing when a company operates across a number of foreign country markets in which not only do the uncontrollable variables differ significantly between one market and another, but the controllable factors in the form of cost and price structures, opportunities for advertising and distributive infrastructure are also likely to differ significantly. It is these sorts of differences that lead to the complexities of international marketing.

At its simplest level therefore, international marketing involves the firm in making one or more marketing mix decisions across national boundaries. At its most complex, it involves the firm in establishing manufacturing facilities overseas and co-ordinating marketing strategies across the globe. At one extreme there are firms that opt for 'international marketing' simply by signing a distribution agreement with a foreign agent who then takes on the responsibility for pricing, promotion, distribution and market development. At the other extreme, there are huge global companies such as Ford with an integrated network of manufacturing plants worldwide and who operate in some 150 country markets. In these latter cases, international marketing becomes a process of managing on a global scale.

Export marketing is seen by many companies as the simplest strategic choice. Global and multinational marketing are more complex and require a revised attitude to international marketing. The world for such companies is seen as a market segmented by Social and cultural/Legal/Economic/Political/Technological (SLEPT) boundaries. In Session 3 of this Companion we examine in some depth these important SLEPT factors and assess their influence in international marketing.

The structure and the way a company organises its activities in international markets gives rise to the alternative forms of marketing operations outlined below. It is this level of involvement that determines the strategic and contextual nature of a company's global operations and thereby the strategic choice it makes:

- **Export marketing:** Often a strategic choice of smaller companies. Where the operations of the company are based in the domestic market and the company purely concerns itself with the marketing of goods and/or services it produces across national/political boundaries.

- **Multinational marketing:** Where the organisation has activities, interests or operations in more than one country and where there is some kind of influence of control of marketing activities from outside the country in which the goods or services will actually be sold, but where the global markets are primarily perceived to be independent markets and profit centres in their own right.

19

- **Global marketing:** Where the whole organisation focuses on the selection and exploitation of global marketing opportunities and marshals resources around the globe with the objective of achieving a global competitive advantage.

Which of the strategies outlined above that a company decides to follow will determine the type of skills and capabilities required of its managers. Often exporting may be chosen as a strategy because it makes less demand on company resources in terms of finance as well as management skills.

Global marketing calls for managers who are capable of operating as international marketing managers in the truest sense, a task which is far broader and more complex than that of operating either in a specific foreign country or in the domestic market. In discussing this, Terpstra and Sarathy (2000) comment that 'the international marketing manager has a threefold responsibility, international marketing (marketing across national boundaries), foreign marketing (marketing within foreign countries) and global marketing management (co-ordinating marketing in multiple markets in the face of global competition)'.

Activity 1.3

Draw up an analysis of your own skills and knowledge in relation to your ability to act as a marketing manager in the following areas:

	International marketing	Export marketing	Global marketing
Strengths			
Weaknesses			

Approaches to international marketing

Firms typically approach involvement in international marketing rather cautiously, as the first step towards what may appear to them to be a rather unpredictable future. For small and medium-sized firms in particular, exporting remains the most promising alternative to a full-blooded international marketing effort, since it appears to offer a degree of control over risk, cost and resource commitment.

The internationalisation of the firm is the process in which an enterprise gradually increases its international involvement. This process evolves in an interplay between the development of knowledge about foreign markets and operations on one hand and an increasing commitment of resources to foreign markets on the other. Market knowledge and market commitment are assumed to affect decisions regarding the commitment of resources to foreign markets and the way current activities are performed. Market knowledge and market commitment are, in turn, affected by current activities and operational decisions.

Thus firms start internationalisation by going to those markets that they can most easily understand. There they will see opportunities, perceive low market uncertainty and gain experience. Then, as they go through the internationalisation process, they will enter new, more challenging markets where there is greater psychic distance. Psychic distance is defined in terms of factors such as differences in language, culture, political systems, etc., which disturb the flow of information between the firm and the market. This means that as the companies' market knowledge grows, so does their commitment, which in turn affects the type of strategy they decide to try.

For many companies, the internationalisation process is not a gradual incremental process but a series of step changes as they become more confident and competent about operating in an international market.

Consider a company that brews beer, based in the USA. The four main strategies for entering an international market identified below provide an increasing level of control at the cost of an increasing level of risk:

- **Indirect exporting** – an example of this would be a trading company based overseas selling beers brewed by the company in the USA. This might be useful as a trial exercise but it is not a practical option for a high volume relatively cheap product like beer, due to the requirements for promotion and distribution.

- **Direct exporting** – this requires commitment and investment in the target foreign market. Not a particularly practical option in the long term because the company still needs to set up a marketing and distribution subsidiary overseas and ship its product across.

- **Co-operation strategies** – include joint ventures, alliances and legal relationships such as licensing.

- **Manufacturing overseas** – possibly the only effective means of competing long term in the overseas brewed drinks market. However, if their brand has low awareness in the country selected then this is a high risk option.

Developing effective relationships up and down the supply chain

In order to make such step changes, firms trying to internationalise their activities put great emphasis on building close relationships, not only with customers but with others throughout the supply chain. Effective relationships are crucial and sometimes the focus of successful organisations' competitive advantage may not be the product itself but the added value given to the product by the close, meaningful and regular communication with customers.

Companies in any market establish and develop relationships through interactions in which the parties build mutual trust and knowledge. The firm is engaged in a network of business relationships comprising a number of different firms – customers, customers' customers, competitors, supplementary suppliers, suppliers, distributors, agents and consultants as well as regulatory and other public agencies. In any specific country, different networks can be distinguished. Any or all of these relationships may become the conduit for the company as they develop their markets internationally.

Activity 1.4

Identify a company known to you that has a highly developed international business.

Discuss with the company management the process by which the company developed their international activities.

Ethical considerations

Consumers globally are becoming better informed through better education, and faster and more effective communications. Increasingly, therefore, they are able to question the actions of multinational enterprises. For their part, whilst the largest multinationals are extending their influence within the global markets they are becoming more vulnerable to criticism. Over the last few years, quality and service have improved considerably but now firms are increasingly expected to ensure that their behaviour is ethical and in the interests of the global community which makes up their market.

Over the past five years Shell have attempted to respond to pressure from global lobby groups and have been much more actively aware of their environmental as well as ethical responsibilities. This has not necessarily been for altruistic reasons but is a growing recognition of the importance of the perception of the global community to companies who fail to take these issues on board. Even so, their efforts did not stop the government of Nigeria in 2001 requisitioning a large amount of equipment and machinery without any prior warning in response to media stories about the company's business practices in Nigeria.

Cultural sensitivity is also often at the heart of the ethical dilemmas faced by managers. There are few, if any, moral absolutes and few actions for which none can provide reasonable justification. Almost every action can be justified on the basis that it is acceptable in one particular culture. In thinking about ethics you should beware of simply defining what is ethical by those standards, values and actions from your own culture.

Although governments, industry watchdogs and organisations often provide ethical guidelines, ultimately international managers have to make decisions based on their own personal views of what is and is not ethical.

In making decisions, ethical marketers need to be aware of:

- Changing societal views of acceptable behaviour.

- How decisions will be viewed by stakeholders.

- The perceived and real impact upon the organisation of making those decisions.

Central to their concerns is the importance the company places on the need for an ethically responsible approach to their operations on the global markets. However, interwoven within this are the commercial concerns of the business.

Companies are increasingly of the view that organisational behaviour considered to be unethical can decrease a firm's wealth whilst behaviour considered by stakeholders to be ethical can enhance a company's competitive advantage on global markets. Conflicts occur often – for example, the economic need to source cheap raw materials against the ethical need to ensure that suppliers are not exploiting cheap labour in producing them.

The consequence of an ethically responsible approach would involve increased resources and attention being applied to a number of areas, such as:

- Need for accurate and timely information about operating practices, suppliers etc.

- Increased attention to press, public reaction and global pressure groups – this is examined further in Session 3.

- Closer relationships with stakeholders and members of the supply chain to ensure all interests are taken into consideration.

- When serious risks are identified then positive and constructive action needs to be taken. From a purely 'business' perspective, should events overtake the company they can possibly mitigate any adverse publicity by demonstrating that they had been taking action.

Case Study – Zimflowers

Encouraged by increasing European demand, and the success of its neighbours (particularly Kenya), Zimbabwe began an increasingly lucrative flower production and exporting industry in the 1980s. Climatic conditions were ideal, and the construction of glass or polythene houses, whilst expensive, was relatively easy. In the early 1990s the success continued, especially in the export of roses. 'Special occasion' purchasing (for example Valentine's Day) made roses a lucrative proposition.

More and more farmers and growers entered the industry, until a number of these regularly supplied the Dutch flower auction market and directly exported to Frankfurt in Germany, and the United Kingdom. Gradually the infrastructure (for example cool stores at the airport) was improved. Exports of cut flowers stood at 3,985 tonnes in 1992/3 and the industry predicted a rise to 8,200 tonnes by the millennium.

The major world exporters of cut flowers in 1993 were the Netherlands (via agents and the auction market) followed by Colombia, Israel and Italy. In Africa, Kenya was a major player, much bigger than Zimbabwe, but in roses, Zimbabwe began to give Kenya cause to notice.

The principle success factors in the growing and exporting of flowers are infrastructure (for example cool stores, cool transport facilities), government support (for example providing a 'climate' for the industry to flourish), importers (for example providing information on prices, demand etc.) and uplift facilities (air transport to major markets). Whilst Zimbabwe has experienced these success factors to some degree it was not as advanced as Kenya (exports in 1992/3 some 16,000 tonnes). In addition, Kenya had other advantages: some growers belonged to multinationals (for example Brooke Bond), and had far better and more frequent uplift facilities to the major markets. Zimbabwe had only one national carrier, which was sometimes unreliable. The country was also served by a few other international carriers (for example Lufthansa), most of which flew North/South. Table 1 gives the comparative air freight rates from selected flower exporting countries, into Europe in 1992.

Country	Air Freight Rates US $ per kg.
Colombia	1.85 + 7%
Israel	1.48
Kenya	1.59 to 2.00
Malaysia	3.46
South Africa	1.85
Zimbabwe	2.00

Table 1: Comparative air freight rates from selected flower exporting countries into Europe in 1992

During the early 1990s there was a feeling amongst the traders that Zimbabwe should be looking for markets elsewhere. This was partly due to more production coming in from competing countries. There was also a feeling in the industry that the growers were not getting as good a price as they could in selling into the Dutch auction, and that with the Dutch re-exporting to other parts of the world Zimbabwe was losing out on some market opportunities. Typically, both Dutch agents and the auction would add 25% to the Cost Insurance Freight (CIF) price. Wholesalers, to whom the Dutch exported, would then add 20-25% to the agent's auction price. Finally, the florists and supermarkets to whom the wholesalers sold on to would set a retail price up to double their delivered price. In this way the final retail price could be 2 to 3 times the original CIF price from the same growing country.

In 1993 the Horticultural Promotion Council in Zimbabwe, a body promoting the interests of many growers, decided it was time to explore new markets as alternatives alongside its traditional ones.

Source: *International Marketing Strategy* examination paper, June 1999.

Questions

1. Choose either other European or ASEAN countries as possible new market destinations.

Outline the factors which the Horticultural Promotion Council should consider before entering the market.

SUMMARY OF KEY POINTS

- International trade is traditionally said to have developed because one country can produce a product at a lower cost than is possible elsewhere (Theory of Comparative Advantage).

- National advantage (Porter) is gained through four major attributes – factor conditions, demand conditions, related and support industries and firm strategy, structure and rivalry.

- International markets are usually categorised into three main types of economy – developed, emerging and less developed countries.

- Organisations operate internationally via exporting, multinationally and globally (worldwide).

- Different approaches require different levels of skills and resources and for small companies exporting may represent a low risk and cost effective means of entering an international market.

- When operating across borders, marketers need to force strong relationships up and down the supply chain based on trust and mutual understanding of each other's needs.

- Ethical decision making is complicated by the cultural differences encountered when operating across a number of national borders.

Improving and developing own learning

The following projects are designed to help you develop your knowledge and skills further by carrying out some research yourself. Feedback is not provided for this type of learning because there are no 'answers' to be found, but you may wish to discuss your findings with colleagues and fellow students.

Project A

Imagine that you work for a small to medium sized firm producing a product of your choice.

What information do you need in order to identify opportunities for entering one or more international markets?

Project B

Having completed your skills analysis, discuss it with marketers who are experienced at working across borders and note priorities for development.

Identify ways of achieving this – it could be through further reading of marketing texts, journals and quality press, secondment, work shadowing, working on a special project or other means.

Project C

Identify an ethical dilemma that a company known to you has had to face. What was the outcome?

Did the company take an ethically responsible approach to the solution?

What was the outcome of their decision?

Feedback to activities

Activity 1.1

In studying international marketing it is important to develop an awareness of the critical events facing companies as they carry out their business activities around the world. It is therefore important for you to be regularly scanning the quality press. *The Financial Times*, *The Economist*, *Business Week*, Wall Street Journal and specialist journals to your industry are the type of papers you should be scanning.

Activity 1.2

You will need to consider which categories you will fit particular countries, for which you can find news stories. For instance, the USA is clearly a developed economy whereas a news story in China would be viewed as an emerging market and perhaps one in Angola as a LDC.

Activity 1.3

This task is designed to give you the opportunity to spend a few minutes to reflect, firstly on the varying type of management resources firms require depending on the strategic choice made, and secondly on the skills, knowledge and level of awareness you may need to build for yourself in pursuing a career as an international marketing manager.

Activity 1.4

In this activity you are trying to identify such things as:

■ The length of time the firm took to internationalise.

■ How they used the partners in the supply chain to internationalise.

■ The impact on the resources needed as they increased their development.

Session 2

Introduction to world trading

Introduction

This Session provides an overview to the international trading environment in which international marketing takes place. It includes discussion on the emergence of world trading groups, potential barriers to success for organisations to overcome and trends and developments in trading patterns.

LEARNING OUTCOMES

At the end of this Session you will be able to:

- Explain the changes in world trading patterns and potential barriers to the development of world trade.

- Discuss the development of world trading groups.

- Identify and discuss potential future changes and developments in world trade.

World trading patterns

Global marketing takes place within the framework of the international trading environment as well as a plethora of complex cultures. It is the first of these two aspects of the global marketing environment that are given priority in the first part of this Session.

Growth in international trade has consistently outperformed growth in world output over the past decade and has been the major stimulus in itself for world economic growth. International trade has been one of the fastest growing areas of economic activity, multiplying at least 25 times since 1945. International trade in merchandise is in excess of US $7 trillion. The triad of Asia, Europe and America accounts for approximately 80 per cent of this.

Europe and the US alone account for 56% of world GDP but only 11% of the world population. This is why developing Asia is so important to the development of world trade. In total, Asia represents 33% of world GDP (including Japan) but it accounts for 59% of the world's population, a huge and growing market.

Barriers to world trading

Whilst countries have many reasons for wishing to trade with each other, it is also true to say that all too frequently an importing nation will take steps to inhibit the flow of goods.

In the last forty years, there has been a gradual reduction in tariff barriers in most developed nations – due to the actions of the World Trade Organisation established in 1984 – but non-tariff barriers have substantially increased. Tariff barriers are the duties and taxes imposed by nations and unions, such as the European Union, on imports.

Non-tariff barriers are more difficult to identify as they are not as overtly recognisable as tariffs. They are often an unknown quantity for the marketer and are much less predictable so can have devastating effects. Examples of non-tariff barriers include:

- Quotas.
- Technical requirements relating to labelling and packaging.
- Financial controls within the importing country.
- Customs practices and procedures.
- Procurement policies (e.g. "buy national").

Fostering international trade

To foster international trade, several world organisations have been developed. The World Trade Organisation (replacing GATT), The World Bank (known officially as the International Bank for Reconstruction and Development, IBRD) and the International Monetary Fund (IMF) are examples of some of the most important ones.

The role of these institutions is to facilitate the development of world trade through the development of an infrastructure that supports trade between different countries. For example, the IBRD supports less developed countries by providing financial and technical help to make them more productive and raise the standard of living. Unfortunately this has led to some of the poorer countries building up a huge debt due to the repayment terms agreed to.

To help poorer countries, the International Development Association (IDA) provides financial support on terms that includes a period of grace so countries can invest in their development before starting to repay the loan. Typically this period is 10 years. Loans are also interest free. However, strict rules apply for the awarding of such loans, which may cause less developed countries further hardships.

International marketers need to understand the role of these institutions in promoting free trade across global markets.

The UK's share of global merchandise exports has declined appreciably over the past 30 years. Compared with a 7.5% share in the mid-1960s, the UK currently accounts for only 5.1% of global visible exports. The pronounced change in the geographical structure of UK exports over the past three decades largely reflects the consequences of the UK's accession to the European Union. In 1970, less than a third of UK exports went to countries that now constitute the EU. Now this proportion is in excess of 60%. The development of intra-trading within regional trading groups is a key development in world trade which will be discussed in the next section.

Activity 2.1

In the illustration 2.2 (Doole & Lowe p.51), entitled 'Scanvaegt – Denmark v the French authorities' an interesting example of a Danish company is discussed.

For your own organisation or an organisation of your choice, identify the markets in which the company perceives it faces major barriers to trade and discuss with the managers the impact of these on the company's operations in those markets.

Regional trading groups

A major trend examined in world trading is the development of regional trade groupings around the world. The recommended reading for this Session discusses the different forms of world trading groups that exist and the varying levels of commitment different types of market co-operation requires.

The European Economic Union, the North American Free Trade Area (NAFTA) and the Association of South East Asian Nations (ASEAN) are particularly important trading groups.

European Economic Union

The formation of the single European market in 1993 was a significant benchmark in the development of regional trading groups. Many of the other trading groups have been formed in some measure as a response to the development within Europe of a single market of 380 million people. The relationship between many of the member countries has been deepened further by the formation of the European Monetary Union in 1999. EMU started with 11 founder members. Denmark and Sweden opted out and the UK has not yet taken the decision to join. The formation of the EMU has impacted on the global marketing strategies of companies, inside and outside the European Union (EU).

The strategic aspects of EMU are, however, notoriously difficult to judge. EMU is not just a monetary event but one that is likely to have a serious impact on the economy. In the long term, prices and wages will become transparent; consumers will shop around for the best deals; middlemen will try to exploit any prevailing regional price differences; margins everywhere will come under pressure.

The competitive environment could also be tougher under EMU. This seismic change will affect companies both inside and outside the EMU zone, except that it will force insiders to adjust quickly, while outsiders might take longer to adjust. Intra-regional trading amongst EU members accounts for 70% of all intra-trade. With such inter-dependency, it is little wonder that so much effort has been put into completing the unified market.

North American Free Trade Area (NAFTA)

NAFTA was born in 1994. The USA, Canada and Mexico created the world's richest market by the creation of the North American Free Trade Area. NAFTA created a single market of 360 million people producing over US $6 trillion in annual output. Their combined intra-trade amounted to US $200 billion and commentators expected NAFTA to add potentially $30 billion per annum to the combined GDP. It is thought that the ultimate goal is to form a Free Trade Area of the Americas (FTAA) and so bring much closer trade collaboration between North and South America.

Association of South East Asian Nations

ASEAN is currently under development. Its members, Thailand, Indonesia, Singapore, Brunei, Malaysia and the Philippines, have agreed to form a free trade area by the year 2008.

This will create a largely tariff-free market of 340 million people. The scheme aims to reduce tariffs or internal trade to a common preferential tariff of 0-5%.

However, some observers are sceptical about the development. Geographical distances and cultural disparities have meant that previous attempts at closer economic integration have failed. These nations are keenly competitive and previously have not kept to agreements to lower trading restrictions. Nevertheless, the Asian economies are pulling closer together than ever before and this trend is likely to accelerate. The next section will consider the current trends and developments in world trade.

Activity 2.2

Prepare a PowerPoint presentation on the implications of the formation of European Monetary Union to a company known to you, that markets its goods and services across the European Union.

Chinese Economic Area

The world is experiencing substantive changes in the global competitive structures as emerging markets strengthen their economic foundations and the regional trading areas discussed above become increasingly cohesive. Europe now has monetary union and is planning to expand into Eastern Europe within the next five years. Free trade areas are emerging in Asia Pacific and the Americas, moving world trade away from global multi-lateralism to a more regionally focused trading pattern and China is developing the potential to dwarf most countries as it continues its rapid growth pattern.

In the decade ahead, the Chinese Economic Area (consisting of China, Hong Kong and Taiwan) is seen by many to be the centre of gravity and dynamism in world trade. This is a prediction that could conceivably fall flat due to political circumstances. The implosion of China being driven by the huge income discrepancies that are emerging within social groups and between regions on the one hand, and the increasingly apparent illegitimacy of the Communist Party on the other, is not a totally implausible scenario.

On the other hand China is now keen to be seen as a respectable player in world trade. It is now a member of the World Trade Organisation and has signed up to the WTO protocols, including piracy. This is a very important step when one considers that 98% of software sold in China is pirated software. The threat of being copied is seen by Western managers as the number one barrier to setting up operations in the country.

However China has continued to experience sustained growth and most forecasters predict this pattern is likely to continue. A study by The World Bank Report – China 2020, estimates that China will achieve an annual growth rate of 6.5% for the next 20 years – which would make it the world's second largest exporter after the US. China's Academy of Social Science (CASS), predict that by 2030 it will have become the world's largest economy, surpassing even the US with a GDP of $155 billion. Some Western studies have even estimated that China's economy will have achieved the top spot a decade earlier than this.

EU expansion

Within Europe the expansion eastwards will potentially have far-reaching implications for companies competing in the European Union. To date, 10 central European governments have applied for EU membership: the three Baltic Republics (Estonia, Latvia and Lithuania), Bulgaria, the Czech Republic, Hungary, Poland, Romania, Slovakia and Slovenia. In 1993 the European Council adopted the 'Copenhagen Criteria' for admission to the EU. These require that member countries attain the following:

- Democracy and the rule of law.

- A functioning market economy.

- Fulfilment of membership obligations.

From an economic standpoint, 5 of the 10 countries pass the test (the Czech Republic, Estonia, Hungary, Poland and Slovenia) which indicates possible admission to the EU for these countries by 2003.

Depending on the country and industry, growth potential in central Europe is extremely high. The consumer goods market, for example, which was almost virgin territory in 1989, has undergone tremendous growth. Sony's sales in the region have risen 30% annually in recent years while Skoda's sales in the Czech Republic have risen annually by 21%.

Many companies view the expansion of EU membership as a major opportunity, but others view it as a competitive threat.

Activity 2.3

Interview the managing director of a company known to you and ask for an assessment of the five major trends in international trade that impact on their company.

What measures has the company taken to deal with the trends identified?

Case Study – Zack and Justin's

Zack and Justin's dairy company was no ordinary company. Founded in 1970 by two rather unconventional friends – Zack Stocks and Justin Reddy, it had grown from nowhere to a £300m turnover, with net profits at £40m in 2000. It had a stock exchange value of £180m when floated in 1990. As the company grew – it now employed 1,000 people – its two founders refused to compromise on their socialist principles. Until recently, the highest paid employee only earned 6 times the salary of the lowest. Employees enjoyed the best healthcare, pensions programme and other benefits in the industry and could also eat as much of the company's products as they could carry away. Moreover it gave 10% of net profits to charity, paid above the going rate for its raw materials which it got locally as far as possible and campaigned tirelessly for environmental issues. Its products – ice cream, cream, yoghurt, cheese, frozen cream and fresh milk had been described in the press as 'some of the best anyone can buy'. By buying some ingredients from former communist countries and some less developed countries, e.g. Cape Gooseberries from Zimbabwe it had benefited favourably in sales to a number of these countries and had, in the process, built an enviable reputation for 'doing things continually beneficial to the planet, mankind and business practice'.

Zack and Justin's products sold in the UK, Asia Pacific (frozen cream), former communist countries and, increasingly into mainland Europe and North America, distributing through supermarkets, small shops, kiosks and in many food counters in department stores. The products never needed advertising – the quality was so good that it 'sold itself'. It steadfastly refused to supply 'own label' for supermarkets and resisted all efforts at takeover by giants like Nestlé, Diageo and Unilever.

However, a recent event triggered off a vehement reaction in the small town in the UK where the company was located. Someone had made a bid for the company at twice that day's share price. Immediately the shares rose some 25%. The small picturesque town erupted in revolt, led by a local celebrity, a very famous international film star, who was determined to stop the takeover. Due to his high profile status, he attracted a great deal of press, television and other media coverage, plus he had powerful political friends in high places.

On a strictly economic basis the takeover made sense – the shareholders would benefit as it would allow Zack and Justin's to achieve its full international sales potential. A 'businesslike' multinational would be likely to cut some of company's more philanthropic activities like sponsorship of the local radio station, local county fairs and the town's rather less than spectacular football team. However, the company character would undoubtedly change and the local celebrity feared the demise of the truly 'noble enterprise'. His campaign, which included a web site, 'Save Zack and Justin's', appeared to be successful. He had gathered thousands of messages of support, had established a 'fighting fund' of £100,000 and even some of the company's likely creditors had decided to back off. It was a classic case of 'clinical big business' versus 'locals with a heart'. Corporate culture was at stake.

The board of Zack and Justin's dutifully met to consider the bid.

Source: *International Marketing Strategy* Examination paper, December 2000.

Questions

1. As a Marketing Consultant advising the board of Zack and Justin's, analyse all the strategic options (specifically international) open to the company. What factors should the company take into account in evaluating these?

2. Based on this evaluation, what advice would you give the company?

SUMMARY OF KEY POINTS

- International trading is a growing area of economic activity with new trading areas emerging such as China, Hong Kong and Taiwan.

- As tariff barriers are decreasing, non-tariff barriers are increasing.

- Non-tariff barriers are not as overt as tariff barriers and can be difficult to identify and overcome.

- The development of world trading groups has implications for the marketing manager in terms of how they foster and facilitate world trade.

- Future changes and developments in world trade will include new entrants into the international market from current under-developed countries as they clear debt problems and organise their economies and infrastructure.

- Other fast-growing economies such as China will make the international market even more competitive.

Improving and developing own learning

The following projects are designed to help you develop your knowledge and skills further by carrying out some research yourself. Feedback is not provided for this type of learning because there are no 'answers' to be found, but you may wish to discuss your findings with colleagues and fellow students.

Project A

Visit www.divinechocolate.com to read the story of how cocoa growers in Ghana have formed a co-operative to get more value from their crop and the formation of the Day Chocolate Company.

At present the higher tariffs imposed by developed countries on manufactured goods than on raw materials means that it is much more expensive to bring chocolate into the EU than cocoa beans. This makes it uneconomic to manufacture the chocolate in Ghana for export – thus preventing the growers from getting even more value.

What are the implications of this and how might you resolve the situation?

Project B

Visit www.wto.org and note what resources are available to international marketers.

In particular check out the news and resources pages.

Project C

Visit www.economist.com and search the archives for news on any of the issues that you are particularly interested in after studying this Session.

Alternatively simply enter 'international trade' in the search window and see what matches you get! Also click on 'Global Agenda' in the About Us box and Markets and Data at the bottom of the page.

Feedback to activities

Activity 2.1

Scanvaegt had to overcome obstacles that the French authorities had mounted to protect their own companies from foreign competition. This highlights the difficulties that many companies are still finding in the European Union, which is theoretically free from all trade impediments! Think about similar barriers faced by your company. In your answer, review whether your company considers tariff barriers as much less of an obstacle than the non-tariff barriers you identify.

Activity 2.2

In forming full monetary union, the characteristics of the single European market have been combined with the harmonisation of economic policy. Member countries are now expected to pursue common fiscal and monetary policies. This means a synchronisation of money supply, interest rates, regulation of capital market, and taxes. In effect, an economic union calls for a supranational authority to design an economic policy for an entire group of nations. This has many implications for marketing across the European Union. This will impact on companies in the UK irrespective of whether the UK ultimately decides to join.

Activity 2.3

In your interview try to consider a number of the wider issues occurring in the international trading environment, especially current political and economic events occurring globally that may affect the company concerned. You may wish to consider some of the issues you identified in Activity 2.1.

Session 3

The environmental factors

Introduction

The essential difference in the marketing approach of a multinational company to the company in its domestic market, is that the latter is dealing with a known and often stable environment. Knowledge gaps can be plugged easily as the information needed is often readily available. A company operating in international markets has many more complexities to deal with. This Session discusses the frameworks that international marketers use to scan the environment when planning strategic decisions. It also highlights the development of specific pressure groups and their potential impact on planning.

LEARNING OUTCOMES

At the end of this Session you will be able to:

- Explain and use the SLEPT factors to assess international markets.

- Identify the role of pressure groups in global markets.

- Discuss the effect of the C factors on international marketing planning.

The SLEPT factors

For a company to operate in its own domestic market there are considerable difficulties in understanding and in forecasting the future facing the company. In international markets, because knowledge demands are greater and the intuitive understanding, achieved through long experience in the marketplace, varies between country markets, it is exceedingly difficult to obtain a comprehensive understanding of the relevant market environment.

From an international marketing perspective it is useful to categorise the elements of the environment into Social/cultural, Legal, Economic, Political and Technological forces (SLEPT). These are now considered individually.

- **Social and cultural issues** are often cited as being the biggest barrier to successful global marketing strategies. Often the force a company has to deal with may not necessarily be another competitor but the cultural traditions of the country. The next Session of this Companion discusses the impact of culture on international marketing strategies.

- **Legal systems** vary both in content and interpretation. A company is not just bound by the laws of its home country but also by those of its host country and by the growing body of international law. Firms operating in the European Union are facing an ever increasing number of directives which affect their markets across Europe.

  This can be an opportunity or a challenge. Increasing media restrictions and the acceptability of particular creative appeals, for example comparative advertising, can limit the options available in creating a pan-European creative appeal. However, new safety directives in lighting for hazardous areas provided a Europe-wide marketing opportunity for a small manufacturer of safety lamps in South Yorkshire, England. The lamps manufactured by the company were one of the few sold in the European Union that met all the new criteria. This gave the Yorkshire company a head start over their German competitors.

- **Economic forces** were discussed in Session 1. As previously mentioned, it is important for the international marketing manager to have an understanding of the economic forces impacting on the markets in which the company trades. This means understanding the issues at a global trading level as well as foreign country market level.

- **Political forces** are not necessarily an important variable in researching potential in a domestic market. However, in international marketing the degree of political instability in a market is a key assessment criteria for companies evaluating the attractiveness of potential international markets. However, even in politically stable countries, a government may introduce policies that seriously impact on the viability of a market for a company exporting to that market.

  For example, in March 2002 President Bush instigated punitive tariffs on imported steel products to the USA and so jeopardised the international marketing strategies of many European manufacturers. Many sceptical Europeans viewed this as a measure not necessarily to protect the US steel industry but one to protect Republican votes in forthcoming elections.

- **Technological forces** have a significant impact in the international market. Changes in the technological environment pervade every aspect of the international marketing strategy process and as such have far-reaching implications to the international marketing company. Internet marketing has made global markets accessible to even the smallest company and revolutionised the competitive landscape of the global market.

Across international markets, advanced countries are experiencing significant competition from both emerging markets and less developed countries who are exploiting modern technology and their own low labour costs to compete in markets no longer so protected by tariff walls. In addition to this, technological advances have revolutionised global communications and how companies organise their global logistics as well as how they manage supply chain partners. All these aspects are discussed in some depth in the relevant sections of this Companion.

Activity 3.1

The term 'global village' is used to illustrate the so-called shrinking of the world due to the increase in globalisation. Events in one country have an effect in others, either directly or indirectly. For example, the destruction of the World Trade Centre in New York on September 11th, 2001 has been blamed by retailers in many countries for reducing consumer demand for some products.

As an international marketer, consider what factors might account for the variability of consumer demand in different countries following such events in our global village.

The role of pressure groups

Global communications and the ability of the World Wide Web to draw together people with shared interests has led to the growing power of globally based pressure groups. Such has been the success of a number of these, it is now the case that pressure groups are seen by many global operators as one of the key stakeholders to be considered in international strategy decision making. The role of pressure groups in global markets tends to be to raise awareness of issues of concern. Examples that have received wide press coverage affecting international marketing strategies are:

- The efforts of Greenpeace to raise awareness to threats on the environment.

- The anti-globalisation lobby demonstrating against the perceived dark global forces they see manifested in the World Trade Organisation.

- The anti-child labour movement.

One of the main roles of international public relations is to attempt to manage the expectations and aspirations of pressure groups influencing their area of activity.

A key responsibility is to respond to publicity generated by pressure groups on issues where expectations have not been met.

Are pressure groups an influence to the good?

This issue can be explored in any context but we have chosen to consider child labour.

A result of the pressure group activity against the exploitation of child labour has led to guidelines being drawn as to how to deal with such situations. The nature of the global markets, however, and the concentration of child exploitation in certain markets has led to the guidelines and policing of this issue resting firmly within the more developed countries whilst the main problem exists in those less developed ones.

This means that judgements formed about the organisation and its products in terms of their compliance or otherwise to good practice, are made predominantly by customers whose opinions are grounded within their own cultural experience – that of a developed economy. Therefore, many of the guidelines relating to child labour have resulted from the activity of global pressure groups from the developed world and, as previously mentioned, these guidelines are often drawn up with reference to what is acceptable in their own cultures. It is argued by some that these can sometimes be detrimental to the people they are trying to help. Many families rely on income earned by their children in underdeveloped countries – without this they have no money to buy food. The opposite argument is that children who are working may be missing out on education.

There are many other issues that pressure groups tackle and seek to influence, from animal cruelty to the growing of genetically modified crops. Their impact on consumers depends often on the publicity they attract and the degree to which consumers feel threatened or perhaps emotionally involved in the issue. For many consumers the latter will depend on social and cultural traditions. Different countries, for example, have different levels of tolerance to animal cruelty. During the late 1990s in the UK there was a high profile media campaign against the shipping of veal calves to the continent to be raised in crates. This led to reduced demand for the meat in the UK. However, there was not the same level of concern in other countries. The UK has a cultural reputation for being a country of animal lovers so some people in that country would be offended by images of what appears to be animal cruelty in any way. Similarly, the UK has less tolerance of situations where products are perceived to be unnecessarily tested on animals.

The challenge for the international marketing company is to maximise the opportunities offered by global markets and the economies of scale brought through the increasing accessibility of the global supply chain and so achieve global competitiveness. However, they need to be able to achieve this while at the same time taking into account the power of pressure groups to influence good practice and the need to help lesser-developed countries to stimulate economic growth and raise the standard of living.

Activity 3.2

Discuss with the management of a company operating on international markets the role of pressure groups in the markets in which they operate.

Are pressure groups viewed as a significant stakeholder by the management? If so, in what way have such pressure groups impacted on the behaviour of the firm?

The 'C' factors

- **Competition**

    Across international markets, the competitive landscape is changing as competition develops from both emerging markets and less developed countries. Competition from such markets is now able to exploit modern technology and their own low labour costs to compete in international markets no longer so protected by tariff walls.

    As the competitive landscape changes globally, one of the most difficult assessments for an international marketing manager to make is understanding the competitive structure of markets across the globe, which are often fragmented and geographically distant. Critically it is important to understand not only the power of indigenous competition but also where, globally, the key competitors' interests lie.

- **Country**

    Porter suggests it is also necessary to assess the influence of the country from which competitors originate in trying to understand the basis of their potential competitive advantage. He argues that the national attributes the company has developed based on its country of origin will help it foster a competitive advantage. These attributes could be based on specific knowledge, capital, special physical resources, the infrastructure of the country or its human resources. How a company uses such attributes may well determine its power as a competitor in global markets.

Marlboro cigarettes saw its macho American cowboy heritage as a key selling point and so in their European campaign took their existing US advertisement and simply dubbed it in the appropriate language for the country. In Sweden this was seen as amusing, whereas dubbed into French it was viewed as quite ridiculous that a wizened cowboy would speak in so elegant a language.

Fiat, concerned about the poor image of Italy as a car maker, cleverly turned this concept on its head in their European campaign by showing the Germans spying on it and being in awe of its engineering prowess – thus trying to capitalise on the German reputation for high quality engineering.

Porter also identified that the forces driving international marketing could be divided into currents and cross-currents. Currents are the macro forces such as the growing homogeneity of markets, the drive towards regionalisation, the rise of the emerging markets and shrinking communications. Some of these were discussed in Session 2 and the first part of this Session.

Cross-currents are the emergent trends in international marketing strategies which are driving international competition to behave in new and, sometimes, innovative ways which are changing the bases of international competitive advantage. It is the cross-currents that are the focus of this section as they are changing the way corporations operate globally and the way they compete. Cross-currents are such things as strategic alliances, the growth of marketing on the Internet, R&D co-operation, increasing involvement by governments in international trade, the growth of pirating and grey marketing.

- **Currencies**

One of the specific characteristics of carrying out business across international markets is that often it is carried out in different currencies. Considerable problems can arise because of the need to buy and sell products in different currencies. A company needs to decide in what currencies it should price its products, as well as how it will deal with fluctuating exchange rates over which it has no control. The European Union introduced the single currency of the Euro in January 2002 to alleviate such problems when marketing to participating countries. However for companies operating in countries outside the Euro zone such questions still need to be resolved.

Activity 3.3

Use the C factors discussed above to identify factors that a large supermarket chain might consider before making a decision whether to expand into international markets.

Case Study – Car wars

"A decision in a Detroit boardroom, 2,000 job losses in a Luton (UK) factory – the price we pay for globalisation".

This was the headline in the financial section of the *Mail on Sunday* newspaper in December 2000. That year saw chaos looming in the UK car manufacturing and marketing scene.

Until the beginning of November 2000, there was not the slightest hint that the relatively efficient Vauxhall car factory at Luton, UK would close with the loss of 2,000 jobs. After all, it was only in 1998 that Vauxhall's Chairman and MD had given up his basic salary for a year in order to secure backing for a productivity linked pay deal designed to secure the future of car production at the plant.

Yet the Vauxhall closure was not the only bad news to hit the industry. Despite having one of the most efficient car production plants in the world at Sunderland, in the North East of the UK, there was considerable speculation that Nissan was to move the new Micra production to France; however this has now been averted. Peugeot, the French car manufacturer, was warning that its £50 million investment in car manufacturing at Coventry, the traditional home of the UK car industry, was in the balance. BMW had already sold Rover.

Ford had announced it was to end volume production at Dagenham, near London. Mercedes announced that at the end of 2000 it was to close 40% of its dealers (from 156 to 63) threatening 2,000 jobs. Ford, Fiat and Volvo were all considering the future of their "independent" dealerships and working up a dedicated sales force deal in anticipation of a new EU ruling in 2003 which could end "manufacturing only" car dealerships.

At the end of 2000, only Toyota offered a ray of hope. It had decided to produce a new model on the Derby production line instead of in France. At the end of the year there was a feeling that the industry has seen all this before.

In the 1960s, British manufacturers flourished but complacency, under-investment and poor labour relations left the UK unprepared in the increasingly global marketplace of the 1970s, especially against growing competition from Asia Pacific and Europe. This all changed in the 1980s when government policy encouraged foreign inward investment as a means of entry into the larger European market. EU rules helped by limiting the number of Japanese imports. All looked rosy. So what went wrong?

There were a number of factors. Many car manufacturers were attracted by promises of big state aid to set up in a particular country, even though the numbers did not make economic sense. Now they are wondering what plants to keep! Consumers in the UK were disillusioned by what they saw as inflated car prices and began shopping around in Europe to import at keener prices, sometimes via the Internet. Sales had slowed in the USA and Europe (by some 15%). Car manufacturing, especially in Europe in 2001, was predicted at 18m cars (Source Commerzbank 2000) but predicted buyers were only 15m. Britain, outside of the Euro group, also faced higher exporting costs due to the strong pound.

Manufacturers were having to shift production to newer, more efficient plants in Europe where several models could be made on one single production line. There was a strong suggestion that the new Vectra model, originally planned for Luton by General Motors, would now be made in Germany from 2003. Quite simply there was overcapacity in the industry and the "super" manufacturers like General Motors and Ford could not continue to carry European losses any longer.

The new century was not looking good for Britain's car industry. Globalisation may have its advantages, but it comes at a price!

Note: Information for this case has been collected from a number of public sources. The figures have been adjusted to enable clearer relationships to be observed. The material is not intended to imply good or bad practice. This mini case is presented as illustrative material and is suitable for teaching purposes only.

Source: *International Marketing Strategy* examination paper, December 2001.

Questions

As a Marketing Consultant to a small volume (200,000 units per annum) car manufacturer of medium priced cars which exports mainly to the UK (20% of production) advise on the possible effects on the company of the shifts in global car manufacturing and marketing as described in the case.

You may base the manufacturer in any country of your choice (except the UK).

SUMMARY OF KEY POINTS

- The SLEPT factors are social, legal, economic, political and technological factors.

- International marketers need to be aware of the impact of the SLEPT factors in their domestic and relevant international markets to help identify opportunities and threats.

- Pressure groups operating in global markets seek to support those who have no effective means of representing themselves.

- The moral guidelines operated by pressure groups are largely developed in relation to the cultural values of the developed world which may not be fully applicable to less developed countries.

- The C factors – competition, country and currency – can significantly influence international marketing planning.

Improving and developing own learning

The following projects are designed to help you develop your knowledge and skills further by carrying out some research yourself. Feedback is not provided for this type of learning because there are no 'answers' to be found, but you may wish to discuss your findings with colleagues and fellow students.

Project A

Look at Doole & Lowe, 2001, *International Marketing Strategy*, 3rd Edition, Chapter 1, Figure 1.4 which outlines the major environmental influences on international buyer behaviour. For a country of your choice use this framework to identify the main factors which would have an impact on a company's marketing plan in that country.

You will find this easier to complete if you either consider a smaller sized company or perhaps one particular strategic business unit in a larger company. It may be more interesting to consider a country with which you are not so familiar. In order to obtain the necessary information you may need to discuss this with company managers as well as searching the web for country based information.

You will also find it useful to reread Paliwoda and Thomas, *International Marketing*, 3rd Edition, Chapter 2: Environmental marketing: the 'SLEPT' and 'C' factors.

Project B

Read the dilemma discussed in Doole & Lowe, 2001, *International Marketing Strategy*, 3rd Edition, Chapter 10, (Dilemma 10.3, page 356). This extract illustrates the role such pressure groups can play in global markets and raises issues as to how demands should be met.

If you read this dilemma you will see that the companies Gap and Levi's responded very differently to the revelation that children were working for companies which produced clothing under license. Gap applied the employment guidelines and dismissed the child, effectively restoring the status quo but leaving the child in a worse situation than before. Levi's dismissed the child but agreed to fund the child's education up to the point when they would be eligible to seek employment.

This pacified the pressure group in the short term but one is left wondering what Levi's would do if they subsequently discovered that there were another few thousand under-age employees across other factories they use? Or if there was a sudden influx of employees that were recruited and then declared themselves as underage in order to seek educational support?

Did any of these issue arise during the discussions you held when carrying out Activity 3.2?

Project C

Spend a few minutes to consider how a multinational company would differ in its marketing approach to a company operating purely in its domestic market. Identify six key differences.

Reference can be made to Doole & Lowe, 2001, *International Marketing Strategy*, 3rd Edition, Chapter 1 (page 25) where the challenges to international marketing managers are summarised.

Feedback to activities

Activity 3.1

The events of 11th September illustrated how people around the world are affected by events in our 'global village'. Consumers and retailers alike are going to feel the impact of such events and their aftermath. Both national and international retailers are affected to a certain extent according to how close they are to the event and its consequences. The factors that might impact on consumer demand between countries include:

- **Geographic factors** – The extent to which consumers feel involved in, or affected by, events will affect their buying behaviours and decisions made about purchases. Any uncertainty may cause hesitant buyers to delay and b2b buyers may be subject to further constraints.

  There is a geographic dimension. For example in the case of the September 11th event, immediately following the terror attack, fewer tourists moved between Europe and America. Traditional centres for US tourists such as London felt the pinch, as did New York which is a destination for affluent European Christmas shoppers. But it could favour regional capitals like Dublin, particularly where they are served by low-cost airlines.

  However, there was also a determination on the part of consumers not to let events prevent them from going about their normal life so the effect may be temporary not permanent.

■ **Social and cultural factors** – Consumers exhibit different buying patterns in a recession or during periods of uncertainty. They tend to make fewer capital purchases and spend money on expensive overseas holidays but give themselves more frequent treats by buying inexpensive products such as chocolate or going out for meals. Such treats are often socially or culturally defined so will vary from country to country. What would you spend your money on?

■ **Economic factors** – during an economic downturn, consumers tend to purchase less with debt and even use cash to pay off outstanding debt, such as credit cards and mortgages. Retailers in some countries will feel this effect more than others depending on how deeply economies fall into recession.

Activity 3.2

In the discussion try to avoid having an emotive debate on these issues. What is important is to consider, from an international marketing perspective, the influence such groups have. You also need to think about the number of extra stakeholders a company has to consider when competing in international markets and how this compares to the domestic market of the company.

Activity 3.3

You will have probably thought of some or all of the following:

Countries – Countries that offer potential opportunity may be those where:

■ Consumers already shop at supermarkets or would welcome the opportunity to do so.

■ Labour is cheaper and has relevant skills or the potential to develop these.

■ It is feasible to build the brand.

■ It is likely that profits close to (or higher than) national market levels can be achieved.

■ It is possible to access adjacent markets, etc.

Competitors – It is unlikely that a supermarket, or any organisation, would want to enter mature markets where competition is high so the levels and types of both existing and potential competition will be important. Markets that are most attractive will be those where there is limited competition, the competitive market is fragmented or not yet established.

Currency – The currency in the overseas markets should be fully convertible, as the supermarket will wish to repatriate at least some of its profits.

Session 4

Cultural influences on international marketing

Introduction

LEARNING OUTCOMES

At the end of this Session you will be able to:

- Explain the elements of culture and how cultures are developed and maintained.

- Discuss relevant models that are used to assess cultures and explore differences.

- Discuss the importance of social and cultural factors for international marketers.

The importance of culture in international marketing

Markets around the world are subject to many influences but understanding cultural sensitivities across international markets poses a particular challenge to marketing managers. Whilst it is possible to identify cultural nuances that are common to many country markets, the real difficulty lies in understanding the specific nature and importance of these within the markets your company is operating in. The sheer complexity of factors affecting marketing strategies can be daunting as consumers in different countries have different attitudes and tolerances to marketing communications, operations and tactics. What works in one country may be unacceptable in another. For example, in India the fast food outlets that are successful have used regional Indian influences in the dishes on their menu. Those that have not, have found that Indian pride in its cuisine means that their products are not accepted by many consumers who prefer more traditional fare.

What is 'culture'?

In relation to international marketing, culture can be defined as:

'The sum total of learned beliefs, values and customs that serve to direct consumer behaviour in a particular country market'.

Thus culture is made up of three essential components – Beliefs, Values and Customs. Customs in some ways are overt and therefore easy to observe. However, understanding the impact of the value system of a culture on the marketing of your product and service is more difficult to ascertain. For example, Western Europe is viewed as having more individualistic cultural values than East Asia which is viewed as being having values of a more collectivist nature. This could have an impact on how a company reaches the key players making purchasing decisions. In Western Europe buying decisions could well be taken without any particular reference to the wider family network whereas in Asia buying decisions may well involve all members of the extended family making particular deference to senior members of the family.

Terpstra (2000) identifies eight components of culture which form a convenient framework for examining a culture from a marketing perspective. These are:

- **Language** – both verbal and non verbal.

- **Religion** – including rituals and customs and their dominance in society.

- **Aesthetics** – what is appealing to the eye.

- **Organisation of society** – this includes the role of men and women, the structures within communities and how power, influence and status are acquired.

- **Technology and material culture** – refers to ways people regard their material possessions.

- **Law and politics** – which set the 'rules' by which people live.

- **Education** – which has nothing to do with intellect but more to do with how formal learning is organised and readily available to all.

- **Values and attitudes** – what people hold to be morally acceptable and how they are poised to behave in response to this.

The difficulty in carrying out a cultural sensitivity analysis on a market is that all these components are interdependent. The view of Terpstra is that culture has an important influence on all other SLEPT factors and therefore is often seen as the most problematic of the C factors. The legal system, the politics of a country as well as the way a country is organised socially is dependent on culturally laden values of that society. Thus how a society regards the role of women, the role of the family and the importance of religion will influence its social organisation.

The other problem for international marketers is that cultural values tend to be fairly stable over time and shared by the majority of the population and so difficult to influence or change. This is why as part of any cultural analysis a company will try to develop an understanding of the ways the culture is maintained and developed. It is therefore necessary to develop an understanding of the key vehicles by which values and beliefs are transmitted in a community or country. For example, members may learn through informal mechanisms, such as their peer groups, family members, and through advertising and other marketing related vehicles. These are seen as the key vehicles in many of the societies of Western Europe. A culture is also often maintained and developed through more formal learning mechanisms such as the educational system or religious institutions and the strict adherence to the formal customs within the society. This is much more akin to the vehicles used in Arab cultures.

Activity 4.1

Using the Terpstra framework outlined above analyse the key factors within a culture of a country of your choice and show how these factors impact on the marketing to that country of a product or service with which you are familiar.

Cultural analysis

When developing an integrated global strategy the international marketing manager has to move beyond focusing on the cultural differences and problems and develop analytical techniques for identifying similarities across cultures. In this section we will examine models by three authors, Hall, Hofstede and Wills & Samli.

- **Hall**

  Hall categorised cultures in the context of the communications. He suggested that the main difference between cultures around the world is related to the way they communicate. At one extreme, cultures such as the Swiss with a high explicit content in their communication are labelled as low context cultures where messages can be readily interpreted by many people. In high context cultures the message needs to be interpreted in the context in which it is given because it is highly specific to the people involved, taking account of factors such as age, gender and position in society. This framework can be used to think through a cross-cultural analysis and the implications this has for the different ways companies need to communicate to consumers in these cultures.

- **Hofstede**

Hofstede categorised cultures across four dimensions:

- **Power Distance (PD)** – in high PD cultures power is centralised at the top whereas in low PD there is a much more even spread of power.

- **Individualism** – in an individualistic society people fend for themselves and their own, whereas in a collectivist society people are cared for and supported by the group they belong to.

- **Uncertainty Avoidance (UA)** – a high UA culture prefers to minimise or avoid risk, whereas a low UA culture will be more comfortable stepping into the unknown.

- **Masculinity** – in a culture where masculinity is favoured then status and achievement are revered whereas a more feminine culture will place importance on nurturing.

An example of cultural analysis using Hofstede's ideas can be seen in the core texts Doole & Lowe, 2001, *International Marketing Strategy*, 3rd Edition (Figure 3.5 p.82) and Usunier, 2000, *Marketing Across Cultures*, 3rd Edition (Figure 3.1 p.70).

Hofstede uses power distance and individualism to categorise cultures. The Philippines, India and France score relatively highly in Power Distance (PD). Austria, Israel, Denmark and Sweden show relatively low power distance scores, while the United States ranks slightly below midpoint. In business-to-business marketing, in countries which have high PD scores it may be more difficult to target decision makers in a company due to hierarchical management structures and long bureaucratic lines of command. In cultures which have low PD scores and a flatter management structure it is much easier for international marketers to identify and reach the key decision makers. It is also interesting to note that most of the countries viewed as highly individualistic score relatively low on PD whereas the high scoring countries on PD are viewed as having a much more collectivist society.

- **Wills & Samli**

A third model that is useful in assessing cultures and exploring differences across cultures looks at how open those cultures are to new ideas and new technologies. The speed of learning and the openness of a culture to new ideas will give a good indicator of how open that culture is to innovations and new products, an important segmentation and targeting criteria for international marketers.

Wills et al differentiate cultures on this basis by categorising cultures not only into high/low context but also fast/slow diffusion. The promotional tools a company will use in a high context but fast diffusion such as SE Asia may well include relational marketing techniques and the targeting of key opinion formers. In the low context but fast diffusion countries such as the USA more formal techniques and mass media may be more appropriate.

Activity 4.2

Consider some of the international business negotiations in which either your company, or one you know of, may have been involved.

How did social and cultural influences impact on these?

The consequences of ineffective cross-cultural analysis

For a company to operate in its own domestic market there are considerable difficulties in understanding and in forecasting within its own cultural frame of reference. In international markets, where knowledge demands are greater and the intuitive understanding, through long experience in the marketplace, cannot be true for all country markets, a comprehensive understanding of the relevant social and cultural challenges is exceedingly difficult to obtain.

Lack of cross-cultural awareness can be devastating and lead to business failure. The white face of Ronald McDonald caused offence in Japan where white is the colour of death. Wal-Mart learnt the hard way when the US 'have a nice day' greeting was severely ridiculed on its introduction into their German stores. KFC's chicken products so offended the communities in Southern India they caused violent protests. Social and cultural issues are often cited as being the biggest barrier to successful international marketing strategies.

The development of the ability to empathise with different cultures has to be the key challenge for international marketers. International marketing managers need to develop the ability to look at a market from the viewpoint of the consumers inside – to work as insiders – if they are going to succeed in those markets.

James Lee (1966) used the term **'Self-Reference Criterion' (SRC)** to characterise our unconscious reference to our own cultural values when examining other cultures. Therefore, an issue for international marketing managers when developing marketing plans is, how do they ensure they build an empathy with the foreign market and minimise the impact of SRC.

Some writers argue that the importance of social and cultural factors are becoming much less of an issue as markets become globalised. It is argued by some that global telecommunications, the growth of e-business as well as the level of international travel by individuals have all contributed to the convergence of cultures and a lessening of the importance or significance of cultural differences. Thus the impact of socio-cultural factors is much less now than even a decade ago. It may be argued that the success of the growing band of global brands is testimony to this. However, others reason that global brands only exist in a few narrow market segments and that for the vast majority of markets socio-cultural factors still play an important part in international marketing planning. Examples of successful global brands include Gap, Nike, Adidas, McDonald's, Holiday Inn, Xerox, Kodak and even Manchester United!

Activity 4.3

1. Identify three examples of companies that have successfully built a competitive advantage in international markets by being particularly sensitive to socio-cultural factors.

2. For each one, explain why you think they were successful.

Case Study – Branching out

The licensing business involves the marketing of properties held by a rights owner, be they studio, sports federation or brand owner, to appropriate licencees, usually manufacturers or retailers. But as owners marketing their rights in Europe should be aware, what licensed product works well in New York or Nebraska may not necessarily work in Naples or Nice.

American 'classic' or 'hot' entertainment properties – Peanuts, Pink Panther, The Simpsons and South Park – still dominate the licensing market across Europe. When embarking upon a pan-European licensing campaign, the rights owner or his agent must have a sound working knowledge of the European Single Market.

But of almost equal importance is the need to closely scrutinise the cultural, aesthetic and religious values of any territory in which rights owners wish to market their rights.

The Copyright Promotions Licensing Group (CPLG) acts as licensing agency for some of the world's most recognisable entertainment and sports brands including Star Wars, Peanuts, Pink Panther, The Simpsons, South Park, Rupert Bear, Dream Street, the Mr Men, Dennis the Menace, M&Ms and Euro 2000™.

When fleshing out a marketing plan for such rights it is crucial to recognise the cultural differences that exist across national boundaries. The full implications of these must be carefully outlined to rights owners, especially US ones, so that their expectations can be sensibly managed.

When creating consumer products, packaging or even POS in a European territory, the fact that a licensing programme has proved successful in the US or a European state is an indication that it should do well across the board – but this is by no means a certainty. Generally, core licensed categories such as apparel, toys and publishing sell equally well across Europe as they do in the US. But there are exceptions. For the Sony movie Godzilla, CPLG signed 22 food licensing partners compared to just eight partners signed by Sony Signatures for the same category in the US.

The look and style of core categories can also change between territories. The French prefer logos on licensed apparel to be smaller and subtler – a very un-American approach to a licensed product. Colour concepts for packaging and POS can also prove to be a major issue for European agents. In Spain, packaging that uses red and yellow, the colours of the Spanish flag, is seen as an offence to Spanish patriotism. Meanwhile in Greece, purple should be avoided by marketers as it has funereal associations.

Adjusting a property or product to suit a country's colour preference is a minor issue when compared to a state's religious beliefs. Images of skeletons and ghosts, the central part of the Goosebumps TV show, have conspired to keep the show off the air in all predominantly Muslim states. The licensing of a movie, TV show or book whose star is a cute little pig will similarly have no prospect of success in Muslim countries, where the pig is considered an unclean animal. This strict religious rite kept CPLG from building a licensing programme for the hit movie Babe in Turkey.

Apart from these delicate cultural issues, the advent of the EU single market has opened up a wealth of opportunity to the licensing industry, but has also created pitfalls which can catch out the unwary rights owner, agent or licensing partner.

CPLG expanded into Europe in the early 1990s to provide rights owners with a 'one stop shop' for their European licensing programmes. Rather than appoint separate agents for each country, owners could award CPLG pan-European rights to market their properties right across the continent.

But creating a system of securing licensing partners across Europe is only the first step. Licensing deals must be carefully structured in strict accordance with EU single market legal requirements. A fundamental rule of the single market is that goods and services must be free to travel across national boundaries without trading restrictions. This clearly has implications if you are appointing licencees in different states to manufacture the same product.

However, this basic pillar of EU law is under challenge from some quarters. Licensees, keen to protect their own national markets, are understandably unhappy with licensees from other states exporting similar licensed products into their own country. But so long as the exporting licensee is selling 'passively', namely to a customer that approached them, and not 'actively' by deliberately soliciting customers, then, or so the argument goes, the licensee is acting within the law. The area is a murky one, particularly as it is difficult and costly for parties to prove that the product was being marketed passively or actively.

Rights owners or licensers may also wish to confine a licensing agreement to a particular territory. Such a contractual provision is also difficult to uphold under single market regulations since once a product is licensed in one EU territory, there is nothing to stop that licensee marketing the product through the whole of the EU.

Rigorous EU competition law also plays a major part in regulating licensing agreements. For example, licensers may be surprised to learn that any attempt to restrict a licensee's distribution channels, by perhaps forcing the licensee only to sell the product through gift outlets, could be challenged as anti-competitive. Similarly, fixing a retail or wholesale price for the product could also be deemed anti-competitive.

The full force of EU law could well be brought to bear on the uninitiated licenser. Licensers would do well to arm themselves with best advice before trying to commit their licensees to unreasonable and illegal contracts.

Source: *Marketing Business*, April 2000.

Questions

1. What might be the short- and long-term effects for a company, in its domestic market and internationally, that inadvertently offended national pride or dignity by using an inappropriate colour in its packaging?

2. What might be the benefits and disadvantages for rights owners using a 'one stop shop' for their European licensing programmes?

SUMMARY OF KEY POINTS

- The culture of a nation, group or community is deeply rooted in history, tradition, language and many other environmental factors which lead to an understanding of 'the way things are done'.

- Cultures are developed and maintained because people conform to the norms of behaviour – tolerance of change is slow to develop because of the identity which a culture bestows upon a group.

- The work of three theorists – Hall, Hofstede and Wills & Samli are used in this Session to assess cultures and explore differences. Many more examples are provided in the core texts.

- International marketers must understand the significance of social and cultural factors prevailing within their markets in order to avoid offence and to communicate effectively with consumers.

Improving and developing own learning

The following projects are designed to help you develop your knowledge and skills further by carrying out some research yourself. Feedback is not provided for this type of learning because there are no 'answers' to be found, but you may wish to discuss your findings with colleagues and fellow students.

Project A

Consider the latest blockbuster movies distributed internationally. What social and cultural factors have marketers had to consider when planning the marketing of the film and merchandise in international markets?

For example, title and content of the film – in the USA, *Harry Potter and the Philosopher's Stone* was re-titled as *Harry Potter and the Sorcerer's Stone*. Think of the kinds of reasons there might be for this type of change.

Project B

As an international marketer who has used a viral marketing campaign successfully in your own country, what factors might you consider before deciding how to introduce it to a foreign country?

Project C

Review the social and cultural changes that have occurred in your country over the past decade. What are the implications for new product development and marketing communications?

Have all changes been widely accepted? If not, why not? How might this affect foreign companies who wish to export to your country, or set up a manufacturing or distribution base?

Feedback to activities

Activity 4.1

You may find it more interesting to pick a culture that you are unfamiliar with. A number of countries now have web sites that could be a good start for examining such a question. Two such examples are given below. In completing this task, it is not necessary to find a large amount of information. What is important is that for each of the components of the framework, some insight or interesting factor is identified.

Web Links:

www.censusindia.net
www.dree.org/singapour

Activity 4.2

Personal selling and negotiation between the buyer and seller is an important part of international marketing. It is in this process of negotiation and relationship building where cultural factors can have their greatest impact. Cultural differences in negotiation styles can be the major cause of negotiation failure. Whilst awareness of cultural differences may not be a major factor in negotiation success, misunderstanding caused by a lack of understanding can be a cause of failure in negotiations. Readers should be able to use material discussed in the recommended readings for this Session to guide them in thinking about how a firm may prepare for cross-cultural negotiations.

Activity 4.3

In considering this task you need to think about the influence of culture in international marketing. In tackling markets in which buyers speak different languages or follow other religions the international marketer can plan in advance to manage specific points of difference. Often the greater problem is to understand the attitudes and values of buyers in different countries. This type of difference is not clearly expressed and is capable of being misunderstood; it is a lack of understanding of these factors by international marketing managers that so often leads to failures in international marketing strategies. Search the Internet for the web sites of global brands such as Coca-Cola and Nike.

Session 5

Researching markets

Introduction

This Session is concerned with research and opportunity, so provides some tools and techniques for international marketers to use when investigating foreign markets.

LEARNING OUTCOMES

At the end of this Session you will be able to:

- Evaluate customer buying behaviour in different countries at different stages of economic and political development.

- Use market research to identify opportunities, similarities and differences.

- Discuss the criteria for selecting market research agencies to conduct research in international markets.

- Identify and discuss the range of sources that can be used when carrying out secondary research in international markets.

- Use competitive, absolute and comparative analysis when appraising international markets.

The importance of effective research

Discussions in previous Sessions have illustrated the highly complex environment in which the international marketing manager operates.

This Session provides the starting point for the international marketing management process in that it quite deliberately sets out to try to help the student provide the marketing research base from which the strategies can be built in that complex environment. Lack of knowledge of foreign markets is one of the first major hurdles an international marketing manager has to overcome. An effective marketing analysis strategy is the first step in overcoming that barrier.

Customer buying behaviour in different markets

Having read the suggested core texts you will have gained some understanding of the marketing research process and the role it plays in the development of international marketing strategies. This Session will help you identify the different stages in the marketing research process as well as the problems and issues marketing managers need to be aware of in analysing cross-cultural consumer behaviour.

A major first task in international marketing analysis is to evaluate and understand market opportunities and customer buying behaviour in different countries at different stages of economic and political development. In carrying out this task, international marketing managers endeavour to find some mechanism to help them prioritise the markets that offer the most opportunities for their company and give them insight into customer buyer behaviour. The different factors that contribute to this are outlined below.

Level of market development

Gilligan & Hird (1985) developed a matrix that is useful in helping firms to conceptualise the differing types of market opportunities and their requirements regarding the marketing task if competitive advantage is to be gained. It is also a useful linking mechanism to show how the greatest opportunities go together with the greater risk, uncertainty and cost, but potentially the greatest profits. In this matrix, markets are evaluated by level of market development and classified as being either existing, latent or incipient.

Existing markets will have a fully supporting market infrastructure, intensive competition and a consumer who is educated in the products and so is only likely to be responsive to a new entrant if it is particularly innovative in some way.

Latent markets are often found in emerging economies where there are rising levels of disposable income and a hunger amongst consumers for new products.

Incipient markets are difficult to ascertain as they are the markets that do not necessarily exist in the short term; perhaps the countries have been unstable politically and economically or at low levels of economic development. However, from your assessment you have evaluated that conditions are beginning to emerge that lead you to believe that markets will develop in the future. The problems in such markets are that the consumers will have no awareness or knowledge of the product or service and so need to be educated as to product benefits.

Risk assessment

Another way in which the level of political and economic development can be evaluated is by assessing the level of risk. The Four Risk Matrix (Doole & Lowe) can be used to assess the level of risk of a potential country market. The overall risk can be assessed in four contexts: political, commercial, industrial and financial. There are now a number of global indices that regularly track the level of economic and political risk with countries. The BERI index, the Economist Risk index and the Goodnow-Hanz index are three examples.

A Canadian company, Optcan, is in the business of FSOs (Free Space Optics). This is an emerging technology that transports data via laser technology. The company is considering entering the Saudi Arabian market and so carried out a risk assessment as part of a feasibility study to help them decide whether they should set up a presence in the market. They assessed a number of environmental factors to evaluate the level of risk in the four key areas and concluded the following:

COUNTRY: SAUDI ARABIA						
Risk type	Low	Moderate	Some	Risky	Very Risky	Dangerous
Political					XXXXXX	
Commercial	XXXXX					
Industrial			XXXXX			
Financial		XXXXX				

Market attractiveness

A common practice in evaluating international markets is to classify countries by their level of attractiveness and degree of compatibility with the company. Harrell & Kiefer (1993) developed a business portfolio matrix that helps evaluate 'country attractiveness'. It is a derivative of the GE matrix, which is seen as a powerful tool in helping companies to categorise markets into primary, secondary or tertiary markets based on the degree of market attractiveness and compatibility with the company's competitive strengths.

Activity 5.1

Using the Harrell & Kiefer Matrix (Doole & Lowe, Chapter 4, Figure 4.3: Business portfolio matrix, page 102) plot the international market opportunities of an organisation of your choice in key country markets.

What criteria did you use as a measure of country attractiveness?

The importance of accurate data

In using market research to identify opportunities across international markets the company is endeavouring to develop a cost-effective communication channel between the international markets that alerts them to opportunities globally. In doing so there is a need to ensure that the systems set up allow a consistency in their analysis to allow comparability across markets, enabling similarities and differences to be evaluated. One of the great difficulties in international marketing planning is the long communication lines between headquarters and subsidiaries. This often causes inadequate dataflow that results in misunderstandings and wrong decisions being made. An effective Marketing Information System (MkIS) can contribute to solving these problems and provide a solid base for strategic decisions to be made.

Market profile frameworks

The 12C analysis framework is a useful tool when developing profiles of international markets. As its name suggests it lists 12 factors beginning with C that impact on the analysis of international markets:

- Country.
- Concentration.
- Culture/consumer behaviour.
- Choices.
- Consumption.
- Contractual obligations.
- Commitment.
- Channels.

- Communication.

- Capacity to pay.

- Currency.

- Caveats.

It helps international marketers to focus not only on the information inputs to a marketing information system but also the type of understanding needed when going on to develop marketing strategies and provides a framework that enables the company to compare similarities and differences across markets.

The market profile analysis framework is an alternative framework. This focuses on the marketing mix implications of the information that has been collected about the international market under study. It therefore helps develop an analysis of a market that, in an objective way, seeks out potential opportunities and provides a framework for the researcher to build a cross-market analysis which is capable of evaluating the similarities and differences across markets.

However, both these frameworks assume that the marketing manager is examining similarities and differences at a country level. It is often the case that in order to formulate a transnational marketing strategy, the marketing manager needs to identify similarities and differences of individual consumers across countries as well as within those countries. Kale and Sudarshan (1987) outlined a process to analyse cross-national segments of consumers. This was called the hierarchical country consumer segmentation methodology. It was developed on the basis that segmentation by purely geographical factors leads to national stereotyping and therefore, companies competing internationally should segment according to consumer characteristics.

Activity 5.2

Using the 12C framework (it can also be found in Doole & Lowe, 2001, *International Marketing Strategy*, 3rd Edition, Chapter 4, Table 4.1 page 107) analyse an international market of particular interest to a company of your choice. Assess which of the 12C factors is likely to pose the greatest problem to the company you have chosen when entering that market.

Selecting market research agencies

There are two major organisational questions which the international marketing manager will need to address in selecting market research agencies:

1. Should the research be carried out by foreign local subsidiaries, or should all marketing research be centralised at headquarters?

2. Should the fieldwork be carried out in-house or by an agency?

If the decision is made by the company to use an agency then there are a number of criteria that should be considered. For example, the research project may call for an expert field agency with knowledge of the particular market. Likewise if the size of the market is quite large it may mean that an agency with countrywide resources is needed. A priority could well be to obtain an independent objective assessment of a foreign country. This could require specialist interviewing skills which one agency alone might not be able to resource, and thus would require the services of more than one agency. If the company is carrying out a multi-country study and needs a consistent research approach across all markets, then an international agency with resources across markets may be much more able to handle the research programme. Often, research in foreign markets requires a local firm that can do the fieldwork, gather data and provide some analysis and interpretation. The selection and management of the agency relationship is significantly important to the success of the whole project.

When selecting agency to work with, a company may choose:

- A global agency that works worldwide.
- A local agency operating successfully in the market it wishes to enter.
- A domestic agency with international offices.
- A domestic agency with international associate companies.
- A domestic agency that subcontracts fieldwork to a local agency operating successfully in the market its client wishes to enter.
- A domestic agency that employs overseas staff.

A company also needs to ensure they go through a systematic process in choosing amongst the alternatives available. In doing this, the following factors should be considered:

- Level of experience of the agency in the markets under investigation – proven track record.

- Number of staff in the agency with the specialist skills required; for example, language, computing, statistical analysis expertise etc.

- The status and reputation of the agency.

- The international profile of their client list.

- Level and access to skilled interviewers.

Once the decision has been made company will need to make sure the agency is given the necessary briefing to ensure a partnership is built between the company and the agency in which both parties are in agreement as to the parameters and expectations within the brief. Thus there will need to be:

- A clear statement of the research problem.

- An understanding of why the research is needed and how the results will be used.

- A clear statement of the budget available.

- Identification of the key personnel who will manage the relationship with the agency.

Activity 5.3

Assume a company that you know has decided to carry out a study investigating the market potential for their product or service in the Guandong province of south-east China.

What type of agency do consider most appropriate? Provide justifications for your answer.

Sources of information

International marketers utilise a variety of information services and sources. The starting point for companies in the UK is either the International Trade Centre of the local Small Business Advisory Service or Trade Partners UK. These government departments provide a variety of information services. The majority of Western nations have similar government sponsored organisations helping exporters to develop information on international markets. A number of different institutions also offer a range of information services from directories, archives of data sources and publications of market research to general and specific advice. These include:

- Libraries – public, business, university etc.
- Chambers of Commerce and Industry – national and international.
- Export Associations and Councils.
- Trade Associations.
- Embassies.
- Banks.
- International distributors and sales subsidiaries.
- Foreign trade organisations.
- Market intelligence organisations.

Online databases and Internet resources

One of the main developments in sources of secondary information in the international domain over the past five years has been the emergence of a plethora of international online and CD-ROM databases such as Euromonitor, Kompass and Informat.

The use of the World Wide Web to obtain marketing intelligence is one of the most important ways in which connectivity can improve a firm's ability to develop international markets. Buying or commissioning market research reports can be a prohibitively expensive business. For a fraction of the cost and in many cases free of charge, much of the same information can be gathered from the web.

The volume of relevant international marketing information available on the Internet is extensive and new web sites are being developed on a daily basis. Many countries are now becoming much more proactive in publishing country market data on the Internet. A large number of companies operating in international markets are developing web sites as an integral part of their international business operations which represent a rich source of data for researchers.

Problems and limitations of secondary data

Whilst the use of secondary data is essential in international marketing research, students do need to be aware of its limitations and some of the problems that occur in using secondary data, especially web-based data. Unless the web site is an internationally accredited source then the researcher has no guarantee of the accuracy of the data. A fairly common complaint is that general country level data can be easy to obtain on the web but that it is difficult to find specific market data that is of particular relevance when trying to establish the best route to an international market.

Perhaps the most frequently discussed issue is the availability and accessibility of quality secondary information in international markets. The collection of secondary data concerning the economy and the business infrastructure in some countries is still new and, even if the data is available, it may have to be viewed with scepticism. One of the reasons for the distortion of data in some countries is the political considerations of governments. Obtaining information that is reliable and verifiable about markets which are regarded as highly attractive in terms of growth potential, such Vietnam and China, is not an easy task.

Activity 5.4

Following on from Activity 5.2, for the company specified, identify a number of sources that would be useful if investigating the market potential for their product or service in the Guandong province of China.

For each one, briefly explain the type of information available from this source and why it would be particularly useful.

Data analysis

In this final section we are concerned with exploring the techniques that international marketers can use to appraise and evaluate the results of their research in international markets – in other words the data analysis stage of international marketing research. This stage must take full account of the objectives of the research and the clients' needs. Many researchers will argue that the methodology to be used should be decided in the first stages of the research planning as it will impact on the questionnaire design and how the interviews are administered.

In analysing data the international marketers will probably employ one of the following:

- **Absolute analysis** – carried out when research has been conducted in a country other than the country of the commissioning company, and that company wishes to build a market profile of that country market. Both the 12C and market profile analysis frameworks discussed earlier are tools that can be used for such analysis.

- **Competitive analysis** – needed in multi-country research programmes when research has been conducted by the company in all or the most important countries where they are represented. The company will try to build a global picture of the competitive profile across the countries. They will try to assess for each market who their major competitors are, their number, the relative size, market share and level of aggressiveness in the markets under investigation. Perhaps most importantly, the company will try to assess the level of coverage in the market by competitors and where there are likely geographical or market segment gaps.

- **Comparative analysis** – useful in cross-cultural research when companies are trying to compare patterns of demand and consumption in different markets, or perhaps develop a profile of the markets using consistent criteria to enable them to build the base for comparison. The analysis techniques and frameworks used in comparative analysis need to allow the researcher to compare, contrast or correlate various factors in the markets under study. Frameworks that allow companies to do this are the 12C framework and the market profile analysis framework.

However, in some international markets, companies may not have the time or the resources to build such an in-depth profile and so use techniques that that will allow them to build a comparative analysis on one or perhaps two criteria.

Some of the key techniques used are:

- **Demand pattern analysis:** Countries at different levels of economic development have differing patterns of demand and consumption. By comparing the pattern of demand in the country under study with the pattern of demand in an established market when the product was first introduced, a comparative picture can be built of other markets where potential has been identified.

- **Multiple factor indices:** This assumes that the demand for a product correlates to demand for other products. By measuring demand for the correlated product, estimates of potential demand can be made.

- **Analogy estimation:** This is used where there is a lack of market data in a particular country. Analogies are made with existing markets – perhaps the

USA – comparing and contrasting certain ratios to test for market potential.

Activity 5.5

Your company has identified Vietnam as a possible market for future development for your company but there is little or no information available. The only way to build a picture of likely demand is to compare the market in Vietnam for your product with either another country or another product.

Discuss with a marketing colleague which of the comparative analysis techniques discussed this Session may be most suitable for your company to use. What problems are you likely to encounter?

Case Study – Knowledge Interact Ltd

Knowledge Interact Ltd., a consultancy specialising in advising organisations how best to make use of their intellectual assets, is a strategic business unit of a large UK based global Information Technology (IT) corporation. Formed in 1996, it grew rapidly into a £15 million operation. The Board then considered the company's next strategic growth direction.

Knowledge Interact Ltd. was one of many organisations which saw early on the power of intellectual capital as contributing more to growth and competitive advantage than the contributions of finance and physical assets have ever done over corresponding periods in the past. The emphasis on raw materials, finance and manpower until the late 1980s saw many companies missing the vast opportunities presented by an organisation's people, process and structures. The Swedish global insurance agency, Skandia, is a classic example. It markets best practice leaflets, manuals and software on internal and external computer networks. Once Skandia had developed an Intranet, intellectual capital was available in hundreds of places simultaneously, giving it a huge potential to lever its earnings and growth. This was witnessed by the fact that Skandia's turnover leapt from £300 million in insurance premiums to £4 billion in less than 10 years.

Knowledge Interact Ltd. went into the business of advising organisations how to unlock their intellectual capital. It sold its services over the World Wide Web, and provided consultants to clients who responded. It was a natural progression for Knowledge Interact Ltd. to start providing more services on the web, including online global branding strategy development services and global e-business research sites, amongst its many other potential activities. It would still need consultants to engage with companies to deliver its core service – that of 'intellectual engineering'.

To aid the decision where to grow next, the company undertook some market research. Basically, it needed to reach marketing organisations with access to web site facilities, and for Knowledge Interact Ltd. itself, it needed a pool of consultants on hand to deliver in-company services. Research showed that North America had the largest number of Internet users in the world (57%), followed by Europe (21.7%) and Asia (17%). (Source: Nua Internet Services, 1998). In terms of online money spent, North America far outstripped anywhere else in the world ($4,930 million in 1998) compared with the next highest Europe ($298 million in 1998) of which Germany and the UK were by far the highest online spenders. (Source: Datamonitor and Yankee Group 1998). However, this data was insufficient for Knowledge Interact Ltd. to make decisions as it was the companies that sold their products online it needed to know about, not the consumer purchases made on the web sites.

The Board of Knowledge Interact Ltd. decided on two things. Firstly, it needed to locate its headquarters outside of the UK and nearer to the 'heart of the knowledge industry action'. Secondly, it needed much more research data to aid the decision where to locate and what services to develop online to help marketers to sell their products and services in a global e-commerce marketplace.

Source: *International Marketing Strategy* examination paper, June 2000.

Questions

1. As a consultant contracted to Knowledge Interact Ltd., provide advice to the Board on the types of market information which it would require to aid the decision on where to locate its new headquarters.

2. What type of online services would it offer to potential web site marketers?

SUMMARY OF KEY POINTS

- It is important to be aware of how customer buying behaviour varies across different countries at different stages of economic and political development. Consumers may exhibit a greater 'hunger' for new products in countries that have previously been classed as underdeveloped.

- Effective market research is used to identify opportunities, similarities and differences in markets to identify the attractiveness of the country for a product or service.

- When selecting a market research agency, consider what knowledge, skills, resources and experience they need to conduct research in international markets.

- There are many sources of secondary data for researchers to use, including many new online databases and web sites, but secondary data may be unreliable, difficult to verify and non-specific.

- Competitive, absolute and comparative analysis are used to appraise international markets. Each has specific advantages relating to the research objectives and to the markets under consideration.

Improving and developing own learning

The following projects are designed to help you develop your knowledge and skills further by carrying out some research yourself. Feedback is not provided for this type of learning because there are no 'answers' to be found, but you may wish to discuss your findings with colleagues and fellow students.

Project A

From the core text, Paliwoda and Thomas, *International Marketing*, 3rd Edition, Chapter 11, read Exhibit 11.6 titled, 'The US must do more to cut deficit: China.'

At the end of this Case Study, the text refers to inroads made by American firms in banking, insurance, shipping and retailing.

Selecting one of those industries, consider the research that a company in that area needs to carry out in order to assess opportunities and 'attractiveness' of China for its products and services.

Project B

Refer back to the suggested reading for this Session – Doole & Lowe, *International Marketing Strategy*, Chapter 4: International Marketing Research and Opportunity. Illustrations 4.1: Kodak's use of consumer research to assess global market potential (page 99) and 4.2: Goodyear global segmentation research (page 105) give good examples of companies trying to wrestle with the issue of trying to develop a transnational segmentation strategy which analyses differences and similarities across countries to form the basis of a global strategy.

In the illustration 4.1, Kodak argues that consumer research is a key element in the process of comparing consumer behaviour across countries, because it can provide insight into how consumers in different markets form quality judgements about a product. It is a good example of how a global organisation is using quite innovative research techniques to give a deeper understanding of the countries where they are attempting to assess global potential.

In illustration 4.2, Goodyear Tyre and Rubber Company investigated the feasibility of developing a segmentation strategy which could be applied globally to their world markets. The requirement was that the strategy would provide a practical base for an international marketing strategy and prove to be consistent and durable. After considerable research they identified three decision orientations which could constitute primary attitude segments when buying tyres: brand, outlet and price. Using these precepts they then used consumer research to develop six global segments. This enabled them to identify global segments and global marketing opportunities.

Use the Internet to try to follow up the results of their research. Start by visiting the company web sites.

Project C

If you do not already do this, start compiling an index of useful sources of secondary information.

Identify what information is available, how it is available and how it can be accessed.

Compare your list with those of other students and your company colleagues.

Feedback to activities

Activity 5.1

The application of this matrix is a powerful aid to the identification of the 'best opportunity' target countries. In tackling the task you may wish to consider a company operating in a portfolio of markets which is trying to prioritise market opportunities. Make sure that in assessing the attractiveness you use criteria that are relevant to the company. You may wish to discuss with company strategic managers the sort of criteria they most frequently use.

Activity 5.2

It is the experience of the authors that students find the 12C framework a useful tool when developing profiles of international markets. It helps the student to focus not only on the descriptive factors but also the type of market understanding required when going on to develop marketing strategies for a country. Do not worry if you cannot obtain comprehensive information. Do try to identify at least something for each section and make a note of the aspects that are difficult to obtain from secondary information sources.

Activity 5.3

In researching such an area you will face many problems. Particular problems are likely to be:

- Lack of secondary data.
- Lack of sampling frame.
- Mistrust of interviewers.
- Interviewee bias.
- Inaccessibility of respondents.

You therefore need an agency that has the resources and skills to find innovative solutions to overcome such problems. However, you also need one that understands your company and with whom you can build an effective working relationship.

Activity 5.4

There are numerous sources that you can make use of. Perhaps a good starting point for your investigation could be the web sites identified below.

www.tradepartners.gov.uk
www.dti.gov.uk/export.control.uk
www.britishchambers.org.uk

Activity 5.5

In attempting to compare/contrast/correlate factors within the market, you may want to consider use of the following techniques:

- Demand pattern analysis.

- Multiple factor indices.

- Analogy estimation.

- Regression analysis.

- Macro survey technique.

These are described in the recommended reading for this Session. You perhaps need to discuss with a company known to you which techniques they think would be appropriate in researching the potential in Vietnam.

Session 6

Developing international marketing plans

Introduction

This Session reviews the planning process and the need to be proactive in the face of the increasing pace of change and turbulence in the global environment. It also considers the potential problems faced by planners in less developed and emergent economies.

LEARNING OUTCOMES

At the end of this Session you will be able to:

- Describe the process of developing international marketing plans.

- Discuss the differences in approaches to international planning between developed and less developed and emergent economies.

- Discuss non-linear approaches to planning, including expert and database systems, emergent strategies and muddling through.

The international planning process

In studying the issues of international marketing planning you should first address the process issues. Your starting point should be to decide which planning approach to use (for example, SOSTAC which stands for Situation, Objectives, Strategy, Tactics, Action, Control). You can use the model from other marketing modules that you are familiar with and apply it to international marketing planning. However, you will be made aware of the need to add further dimensions to a generic planning approach as you apply it to international marketing, having undertaken the recommended reading for this Session.

The diversity in international marketing, that we have discussed in earlier Sessions, makes planning and control a difficult activity to carry out systematically. In the following section of this Session we will explore the ways in which we integrate a common strategy into the action plans in countries that are at different stages of development. In the final section we look at the problem of planning in a rapidly changing marketing environment around the world and the practical steps that might be taken to address this.

The development of the planning process

Consider how well developed your company's planning process is and the degree to which it is:

- Top down – strategy and actions decided by the senior executives.

- Bottom up – actions decided at a local or lower level.

- A combination of the two – objectives set by senior executives and actions decided by more junior managers.

Whilst we suggested earlier that you should use the planning framework that you are familiar with, it is important to consider certain elements of the plan that should receive rather more attention in international marketing. Analysis of world trends is required as well as local changes in all the markets in which you operate.

You must also assess the capability of all your Strategic Business Units (SBUs), remembering that a SBU in a small market may consist of one or two people, whereas your operation in the US may have many thousands of staff. In this case your SBU in the US might be expected to achieve more (but not always!).

Stakeholders are particularly significant for international businesses because of the need to address the differing expectations of the firm. Increasingly, the minority stakeholders of your company such as pressure groups are becoming more powerful because of their ability to communicate better and influence the worldwide image of the company.

The benefits and problems of international planning

In a small company where experience of international marketing is limited, the methods used for planning are often incomplete, too fragmented, or poorly thought through as the firm starts out on its international development. The culture of planning may be weak in a larger organisation too. This may be because of inadequate organisation, varying degrees of support for systematic planning from its staff around the world, inadequate information collection, ineffective communications and the use of inappropriate or only partially understood control systems.

Organisations operating in many different country market environments enjoy many benefits from a well-developed and systematic planning process and this is the subject of the activity below. SBUs of differing sizes and market potential contribute to the firm's overall performance in different ways and so the objectives and strategies must recognise this. Perhaps the greatest challenge is to satisfactorily implement the strategy efficiently by standardising the processes and marketing programmes, whilst also making sure that the strategy is effective in the marketplace by adapting it, when necessary, to the needs of local markets and cultures.

Finally, the company must establish an organisational structure, control mechanisms and feedback systems that ensure that its diverse operations deliver the planned performance and its managers rise to new challenges when they arise.

Activity 6.1

Thinking about your SBU, firm or an organisation of your choice:

- Prepare a diagram that lists the headings and subheadings for the international planning process. To do this, use the format with which you are familiar (for example, SOSTAC).

- Identify the benefits to the organisation of an effective planning culture within the company.

Act global, think local

In previous sections we have viewed international markets for some products and services from the perspective of one global market defined by a cross-cultural customer segment. However, for other products and services, demand is driven by the needs of the local culture or a very specialised requirement (for example, legal or climatic). Consider why these extremes lead to quite different planning approaches.

The marketing of many food products is culturally sensitive and demonstrates these differences. Heinz (US) took over Honig (Holland) in 2001 and the combined company faces the challenge of planning pan-European marketing of some products, such as Heinz tomato sauce – eaten everywhere with burgers and hot dogs – and local country marketing of local delicacies, such as chocolate sprinkles topping in Holland. The managers have the problem of managing their time between corporate and local products' marketing responsibilities, in order to maximise the company's return on investment.

For senior managers, the problem is how to maintain cohesion between all staff, in order to ensure uniform standards, a coherent worldwide strategy, retain a unique vision and purpose but, at the same time, create an operation which has empathy with stakeholders in each host country. They must also consider the differing factors that affect the success of the firm in less developed and emerging markets. Whilst detailed analysis is necessary to appreciate fully the complexities of a situation at the host country level, there is also a need for a clear uncluttered vision, shared by all staff in all its locations, of where the company intends to go.

In practice, highly diversified conglomerates appear to fail to achieve their potential in exploiting the market and creating effective internal working and external partnerships. A measure of this comes from the fact that stock markets typically apply a 'conglomerate discount' of about 20% to the value that is placed on the individual parts of companies such as Philips and Siemens and the estimated total value of the company. There are only a few exceptions, which have been fully valued and are therefore believed to be managed effectively. The most obvious example is GE during the time it was managed by the legendary Jack Welch.

The problems posed in less developed and emerging markets

For most firms the international planning process is concerned with managing a number of tensions and ambiguities. There is a need to adopt a regular, thorough and systematic sequence, but at the same time provide the flexibility which allows more local SBU managers to realise opportunities and address problems when and where they occur. In less developed and emergent economies, the local market opportunities and threats can change very quickly. This might be due to a change of government, changes in the local economy or relevant laws, a decision made by a competitor to enter the market or war which might flare up suddenly in some countries. These events may make it difficult for the local SBU to implement the firm's generic international strategy.

Less developed and emerging markets may appear, on the surface, to be somewhat unattractive target markets compared to those in developed countries, because:

- There is greater inherent instability.

- There are currency and finance problems.

- Varying previous experience has been mostly negative.

- Marketing staff have limited knowledge and skills.

- Many marketing tools, methods and organisation structures will be inappropriate or need to be extensively modified for these markets.

However, they do offer much higher growth prospects to counter the possible greater degree of risk. It is interesting to note that quite often, firms that have the longest experience of working in less developed or emerging markets appear to be more successful when they enter such markets. One such organisation is Asea Brown Boveri, which has successfully built upon its long-standing links in central and Eastern Europe.

For firms from less developed and emerging markets the challenge of entering developed country markets may be a different one. A flower grower from Africa must learn quickly how the sophisticated flower market operates in the Netherlands in order to establish a positioning of quality, technical competence and image, which is likely to be more sustainable than low price. See the Case Study at the end of Session 1.

Activity 6.2

The greatest difficulty associated with the differences in approaches between developed and less developed and emergent economies is the failure of the head office staff and the local subsidiary or SBU staff to understand each other's problems.

Prepare a slide presentation with the title 'Developing an international marketing planning culture within the firm'.

Include the actions the firm should take to address these problems.

The planning process

The traditional approach to planning is to consider it as a linear sequence of activities that need to be undertaken systematically:

Analysis

Strategy development

Implementation

Monitoring and control

This is a logical approach and may be acceptable for the preparation of, for example, an annual plan, a five-year strategic review, or an investment proposal to develop new markets. However, changes are taking place all the time that affect international marketing firms and so, for them, planning must be a continuous activity, including the updating of objectives and strategy and modification of the implementation plan as necessary. For a simple firm, operating in a domestic market, the impetus for changing the strategy and plans might be the result of a systematic analysis. However, for complex multinational firms the impetus for changing the plan could come from anywhere in the planning process, in any of its diverse international markets, and an immediate response might be demanded. For example:

- Monitoring and control – could highlight a reducing market share, or loss-making.

- Strategy development – changes in fashion in the target segment.

- Implementation – the failure or unexpected levels of success of a new product or promotion.

- Analysis – a sudden change in the environment (for example, an economic downturn), new or more aggressive competition.

It is therefore necessary to think of the process conceptually as a number of interlinked elements:

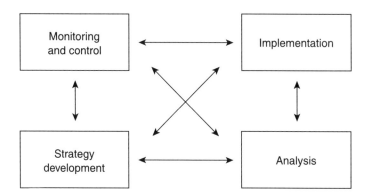

Figure 6.1: The interlinked nature of the international marketing planning process

The need for a faster response

Markets and the environment are becoming more 'turbulent' with more rapid and far-reaching changes taking place because of the greater interdependence of markets and firms. **Evolutionary changes** in the market are taking place more rapidly – for example in consumer taste and fashion, the entry of new competition in some sectors, such as telephones, and faster new product introductions across the world. **Critical changes** such as corporate mergers and alliances, and the introduction of the Euro (the European single currency) are far more significant. Critical incidents, such as the Gulf War, September 11th, the dotcom collapse and the failure of Enron (and the implications for global accountancy organisations) affect more organisations and individuals.

The reasons why the traditional linear approach to planning is not effective is that it represents too long a time span, with the result that the environment has changed by the time the plan has been implemented. This is because the process is too complex. Too many people and fragmented activities are involved in the planning process, too much information, rather than the essential data is collected, and the quality of the analysis and understanding of the implementation priorities is inadequate. Finally, the monitoring and control systems are not sufficiently responsive to identify new trends at the earliest possible time as they occur around the world.

New approaches to planning

More progressive firms are recognising the need to reduce the time between data collection, analysis, decision making and the implementation of changes to the strategy. They are making better use of environmental scanning and their own market information from databases (for example, 'datamining' to enable early identification of trends, threats and opportunities). Decision support systems are in place so faster and better informed decisions can be made. Emergency planning systems exist so evolutionary changes can to be incorporated into the plan. In the case of planning that is designed to allow incremental changes to be made at a local level it is, of course, important to ensure that the SBU managers are properly equipped to work in this way.

Activity 6.3

The airline industry has been dramatically affected by the events of September 11th, 2001 – for example, the failure of some airlines such as Sabena and huge job losses in most large national airlines. However, there has also some reported growth in low-cost airlines such as easyJet and Ryanair.

Some experts argue that evolutionary changes in the industry and critical decisions made both by governments and firms were the underlying reasons for the need for change in the industry; and that September 11th simply accelerated this change.

Taking the industry sector of your own organisation or one of your choice:

1.   Identify the evolutionary changes, critical decisions and critical incidents that have occurred over the last three years and affected the planning process.

2.   What information systems have been used (or could have been better used) to more quickly identify the changes taking place and so improve the planning process?

3.   To what degree has your firm responded to the need for a more rapid response to changes in the market?

Case Study – INDECO (PVT) Ltd

'Economic Structural Adjustment Programmes' (ESAPs) have been a feature of many Less Developed Countries (LDCs). Mainly World Bank sponsored, ESAP was introduced for a number of reasons: severe balance of payment difficulties, inability to service external debt, inappropriate domestic policies (for example subsidies), closed markets, state controlled prices and uncontrolled and increased government spending. Added to this, many LDCs have experienced poor public sector management, idle and decaying industrial capacity and inadequate resources of foreign exchange for materials and spare parts, leading to poor quality goods and services and over-valued currencies.

Africa has been the recipient of adjustment monies for many years (US $20 billion plus). Zambia is one such recipient country. It has experienced both the positive and negative aspects of the implementation of ESAP. On the positive side the economy has 'opened up' resulting in a flood of foreign imports (due partly to domestic producers' lack of quality) and foreign direct investment due to free exchange rate regimes. Certainly more traders have entered the marketing system due to lower taxation cuts.

However, Zambia has suffered many negatives from the ESAP process. Devaluation (500%) has made imports expensive and imports have affected domestic production, resulting in unemployment. Domestic prices have risen rapidly due to inflation and the national debt has risen dramatically. Socially, the populace has become divided with the rich getting richer and the poor poorer. Meanwhile, the government has divested itself of many state owned industries, these having been sold to international investors, making Zambians feel that the Government has 'sold off the family silver' to outsiders. Petty and serious crime have increased.

Within this scenario INDECO (the Indian Engineering Company) based in Bangalore, India, has been exporting standard products (nuts, screws, bolts, washers, clips etc.) to Zambia for the past 10 years through a local agent. Turnover has steadily increased to its current level of US $2 million (2001), but in latter years its margins have been eroded due to the devaluation of the Zambian Kwacha and the inability of local industry (textiles, light engineering, brewing and agribusiness) to source foreign currency to pay for imports. The major Zambian industry, copper mining, is however relatively wealthy. Some years ago, INDECO ventured into Zambia directly by entering into an agreement for a local company to manufacture its products under licence. However, after three attempts to get it right it had to abandon the project, due to the company's inability to manufacture to required quality standards. The local company just could not afford to import the specialist machinery. Such was the importance of the Zambian sales to INDECO, and the potential wealth due to so many South African companies now investing in Zambia (albeit a lot of it in trading), that it was worth INDECO considering venturing into Zambia again. The Board of INDECO met to consider the project.

Source: *Planning and Control* examination paper, June 2001.

Questions

Assume that the decision has been taken for INDECO to enter the Zambian market again.

As the Marketing Analyst write an International Strategic Marketing Plan for the Board, covering the years 2002-2004, based around one direct market entry of your choice.

SUMMARY OF KEY POINTS

- When developing international marketing plans similar tools can be used to those employed by other strategic planners. However, additional factors relating to the international capabilities of the parties involved must be taken into account.

- International marketing planners must be aware of cross-cultural issues when making decisions about planning and implementation of plans.

- Marketers need to take different approaches to international planning in developed and less developed and emergent economies to account for differences in stages of development of communications, technology, country infrastructure and culture.

- Developing international marketing plans is a complex process of interlinked elements due to continual environmental change that demands flexibility and adaptability.

- Planning demands flexibility and speed of response which differs from the more traditional, logical sequential process.

Improving and developing own learning

The following projects are designed to help you develop your knowledge and skills further by carrying out some research yourself. Feedback is not provided for this type of learning because there are no 'answers' to be found, but you may wish to discuss your findings with colleagues and fellow students.

Project A

For a product of your choice, or one made by your organisation, make a decision about market entry in another appropriate country.

Note what data and information you would need to gather and how to analyse this.

Select and justify a market entry method.

Project B

For the product in Project A, determine objectives, strategy and implementation plan for market entry.

Concentrate on strategic rather than operational issues.

Project C

For the same product, identify appropriate methods of monitoring and control for your plan.

Feedback to activities

Activity 6.1

In completing the activity you need to:

- Decide which planning model you will use and how you need to add sub-headings to it to ensure all the international dimensions are covered.

- Make sure that you can use the model for your own organisation and also for Case Study analysis.

- Be prepared to address issues such as international stakeholder expectations and standardisation/adaptation issues as well as your approach to integrating individual country plans.

- The benefits should include: ownership of the strategy and actions by all staff – thus greater commitment and easier communication – speaking the planning language, and faster response by the firm to changes sweeping across the world.

Activity 6.2

Use bullet points to highlight the key points and refer to examples which you would relate to your audience if you were presenting this orally.

You should also make suggestions for improvement under various headings. These might include the McKinsey 7S framework (Doole & Lowe page 161), as well as referring to cultural sensitivity (refer back to Session 4) and communication.

Activity 6.3

You should think about:

- The systems that are used to collect the information from the environment, your customers and your competitors quickly and effectively, their timeliness, accuracy and ease of analysis.

- The decision process you use in the company.

- The way that changes are made to your long- and short-term strategy.

- How the changes are communicated to staff and of effectiveness of communication strategies used.

Session 7

The people factors

Introduction

Planners do not always consider the people factors to the same extent as other elements in the planning process. Therefore, this Session concentrates on how this resource should be included strategically and operationally in international plans.

LEARNING OUTCOMES

At the end of this Session you will be able to:

- Explain the characteristics of a learning organisation.

- Identify and explain organisational and management issues pertinent to export globalisation spectrum decisions

- Describe the measures for managing and controlling in-house and external resources – expatriate, national and global staff.

What is a learning organisation?

Sinkula et al (1997) identified three key characteristics of a learning organisation: the commitment to learning, open-mindedness, and a shared vision.

- **Commitment to learning** – central to a firm's ability to achieve a positive marketing orientation in international markets is the commitment of the firm towards learning. It is this that determines the value placed on the outcomes of learning and willingness of the firm to commit the necessary resources to understanding what is happening in international markets. Learning-efficient companies are reflective and value the need to understand the causes and effects of their actions.

- **Open-mindedness** – when organisations are prepared to constantly and proactively question long-held routines, assumptions and beliefs, they are engaging in the first phase of learning, which is at the heart of organisational change. In an unstable and unpredictable international marketing environment, such a capability is important in enabling a company to respond to competitive challenges in international markets.

- **Shared vision** – the concept of a shared vision has been viewed as the foundation for proactive learning. It provides direction and a focus for learning that fosters energy and commitment. Learning organisations are proactive in identifying the potential offered by trends and developments.

It is this foresight that gives the firms the strategic direction to build a superior competitive position in international markets and helps them move beyond the short-term view of the firm's current markets. The importance of a clear foresight, shared by the staff and management of the firm, is also critical if the company management is to gain the necessary commitment from company stakeholders and staff to carry out the resource-intensive activities necessary to build an international presence. In a learning organisation therefore, the company leadership will have the ability to communicate a well-crafted vision for the organisation and personally motivate and instil a learning orientation in the staff of the company.

Morgan, Katsikeas, & Appiah-Adu (1998) argued that organisational learning capabilities helped firms sustain a competitive advantage over the long term in two ways.

- Firstly, by minimising the incidence and potential impact of serious environmental disturbances, through advance acquisition of knowledge.

- Secondly, by the flexibility, built through organisational learning, to enable the firm to develop rapid company responses in order to exploit emerging opportunities or extinguish threats.

Thus a critical characteristic of a learning organisation is that it has the capability to develop appropriate responses to the strategic challenges faced in their global markets and so are able to refocus their strategic thinking as the competitive challenges in the market require.

Types of learning

In the strategy development process of international firms, two types of learning activity are necessary:

- The learning necessary to signal critical developments and trends.

- The learning necessary to reflect, re-evaluate and respond – 3R learning (Doole 2000).

Signal learning is concerned with monitoring and maintaining a position in international markets. The **3R learning** (reflect, re-evaluate and respond) occurs in response to critical events in international markets when companies question long-held assumptions about themselves, their customer base and their strategic focus. It requires the development of a new way of looking at the world. Thus, it is not merely about adaptation, but challenging traditional assumptions, reflecting, evaluating the new learning and responding with newly developed strategic thinking.

Activity 7.1

What evidence can you offer from the activities of the last twelve months that your company exhibits the characteristics of a learning organisation under the headings:

- Commitment to learning.

- Open-mindedness.

- Shared vision.

Alternative organisation structures

Effective organisations ensure that their culture and structure are mutually supportive. If a company wishes to develop a culture that encourages internal and external learning then its structure must support this. A bureaucratic structure might limit the rate of learning, whereas a matrix structure that facilitates the free flow of ideas and information would enable the organisation to be a much more successful learner.

An appropriate organisation structure is also essential to ensuring that the company's planning and implementation activities can be carried out efficiently and effectively. It is vital that all staff in all locations understand their line management responsibilities and are clear about who they should report to and which staff they manage. An effective organisation structure enables decisions to be made quickly, communications to reach the staff that need to be informed and direction and controls to be applied to all the firm's diverse activities. The structure also sends out a clear indication of the firm's priorities and intentions.

The management decisions facing early stage international companies are relatively simple, but still significant, and the chosen organisation structure sends out signals both internally and externally. Small companies must simply decide whether to set up a special department to handle exports or include exports within the general management of the firm.

As business develops, so different market requirements and internal pressures force changes in the organisational structure. Typically the company might chose to organise by setting up individual operations as profit centres in the various countries in which it operates. Alternatively it might decide to set up profit centres based on the worldwide marketing of a product category or brand. Either will affect the day-to-day decisions made by the staff.

Many companies feel that neither of these approaches is entirely satisfactory and choose to adopt a matrix approach. In this case the operations staff have to report performance to both a local country manager and a head office product category or brand manager, and of course, conflicts arise.

Organisation and management issues in more complex organisations

As the organisation grows, its structure must respond as the roles of managers are constantly adjusted to meet new marketing challenges. It needs to be able to manage the performance of individual managers, no matter where they are located.

As competition increases, organisations are being forced to become more efficient by reducing costs and to become more effective in adding customer value. The organisation structure must avoid duplication and bureaucracy and, instead, constantly seek to encourage innovation. People must be flexible and adaptable in their approach to work and look for new and better ways to operate.

The complexity of these organisational issues is greatest in transnational companies, where the organisation structure takes on an entirely new dimension with advanced forms of networking and matrix organisation structures. Majaro (1991) identified three basic structures in the very largest multinational enterprises (MNEs). Typically, managers at the higher levels of the organisation have a very wide span of control for very diverse activities and their challenge is to deal with the often conflicting demands from product and country operations for time and resources.

Activity 7.2

Draw the international organisation chart for your organisation, or one you know well.

Where are the points of power and decision making?

> Given the nature of your industry, does the structure make it easy or difficult to obtain timely decisions, make effective use of resources and respond rapidly to customer needs?

Managing resources in a transnational organisation

As companies become larger they adopt the characteristics of transnational organisations and typically become more diverse as they struggle to combat fragmentation. Decisions become more complex as a wider range of business and cultural factors have to be taken into account. Partnerships with outside organisations for new product research and development, supply chain development and distribution can mean that sometimes the transnational organisation is co-operating and sometimes competing with the same company.

Organisations in the IT sector are faced with the continual problem of the need to develop products and services based on a rapidly changing and expanding range of technology, each of which is extremely expensive. To invest in all the related technology is now beyond the scope of any single organisation. As a result, companies such as IBM have embarked upon a wide range of joint ventures and partnerships with organisations with which they compete. This calls for different styles of management within the organisation, different roles for managers and, because of the situations in which they are placed in the course of their work and their high profile, increased pressure on managers to behave ethically at all times.

One of the main challenges for the transnational organisation is to encourage local staff to retain their enthusiasm and entrepreneurial activity, essential for growth, whilst at the same time ensuring that they work to deliver the organisation's strategic objectives in an approved manner. We have already discussed the fact that different cultures have different standards and values. In a complex, diverse organisation an important management challenge is to allow local opportunities to be pursued in a manner that meets the standards and values of the firm but also is responsive to the standards and values of the local business and social culture. Successful transnational organisations learn how to gather local feedback and use it effectively centrally in order to 'think global and act local'.

An example of this is that McDonald's adapted their menus when they opened outlets in India to reflect local cuisine. Other fast food chains did not and failed to attract customers, such is the cultural and social importance of the local cuisine.

Expatriates or local managers?

In order to manage this potential conflict, MNEs typically use a combination of staff that are expatriates (originating usually from the headquarters country), local national staff and global staff who typically have experience of living and managing in a number of countries. There are, however, some disadvantages of using non-national staff, typically because of the cost of re-location and higher salaries to compensate for living away from their home country. Some expatriates tend to fit so well into their 'adopted' country culture that they 'go native' and no longer perform the special role of headquarters representative.

Some MNEs give short-term assignments (such as for three or six months) to managers to work in foreign countries to give experience and strengthen the link to headquarters. Quite often this is used when a new office or subsidiary is being established, but there are disadvantages in this. In high context cultures this is not effective because just when the manager on a short-term assignment has built up relationships and a position of trust with potential local clients, the manager goes back to head office to be replaced by another manager.

Research suggests that local, national staff – if properly recruited, trained and given appropriate experience – make the best managers in the local country, as usually they have a better appreciation of the cultural sensitivities and the way that business is really done.

There are exceptions, of course, as some international managers can develop an empathy with the local market and at the same time bring a global perspective. As firms increasingly seek globally to develop partnerships and networks, the skill of making connections becomes vital.

Supporting expatriate staff and their families

Selecting and then supporting someone to work in a foreign country requires a lot of thought and prepared support structures. Often, staff are asked to uproot not only themselves but also their families and this can cause additional pressures and costs such as:

- Children's education – is it best to send children to a boarding school in their country of origin, to a local school or to a local school for their own culture?

- Spouse – will they be able to work? What support is available to them?

- Remuneration – will the organisation support purchase of goods which need to be imported from the country of origin (which often carry a price premium)? Will salary be based on local or home country conditions?

- Housing – does the organisation pay for accommodation so that the jobholder can maintain a property in their home country? If not, then how will the jobholder be repatriated?

- Induction and cultural training – in the language, how to go about everyday life, culture – is this available to the whole family or only to the jobholder? If only to the jobholder, how will the spouse be able to cope?

- Repatriation strategies – what transition arrangements can be put in place for returning families to ease culture shock? Does the jobholder have a guaranteed role back in their country of origin after a certain time?

Organisations often gain significant advantage from having people from their country of origin on site who understand the concerns and culture of the parent organisation; the support required for such individuals can be high.

Activity 7.3

Complete the chart set out below to identify the advantages and disadvantages for the individual and the organisation of working outside own national borders, either by:

a. Interviewing a manager in your own organisation who is working away from his or her own country, or

b. By reviewing business press interviews with senior executives in an international organisation who are working away from home.

	Advantages	Disadvantages
For the individual		
For the organisation		

Case Study – Reputation matters

When you're the underdog, it's easy to attract admiration and encouragement. So it was with Microsoft just over a quarter of a century ago, when Bill Gates and Paul Allen got together to make personal computer software that was more accessible.

For anyone struggling with the impenetrable systems that the giant IBM dominated the market with, this was a welcome innovation.

How things change. In the past few years, the very success of the company has attracted almost unprecedented opposition, fuelled by a high profile anti-trust court case in the US, and accusations that Microsoft is the embodiment of a modern day bully monopoly. Even more woundingly, the company was accused of 'not getting' the Internet until long after others had jumped on the bandwagon.

But the last year has shown that if the $25 billion company is anything, its resilient. An article in *Fortune* in June 2001 entitled (rather aptly) 'The beast is back' argued that a stream of new product offerings and a re-organisation of the way the company does business show that Microsoft has reinvented itself not only in terms of creativity but also in the way it listens to customers.

This is certainly the take on Microsoft that its UK marketing director, Oliver Roll, would agree with. He took over as the company's first UK marketing director in June 2001, having previously been marketing director of Enterprise Marketing. Until then marketing had been devolved across the business. Now, in a model being replicated around the world, marketing has been overhauled to reflect both a desire to be more customer-centric but also to make sure the key messages are no longer diffused.

In its current guise Microsoft operates through four main divisions. First is its desktop business, consisting of productivity software such as the ubiquitous Windows and Office, with Windows XP and Office XP the newest incarnations of the Windows family. This has long been the mainstay of the business, accounting for about three-quarters of revenues at $18 million.

Then there is the relatively new market sector of enterprise software aimed at helping organisations run their infrastructure. This however brings Microsoft up against established players such as Oracle, Sun and IBM, so it will have its work cut out. The business is currently worth $3.2 billion. Nevertheless, Roll believes that within two years it will become the new cash cow as businesses began to embrace the Internet to reach out to their customers, partners and suppliers.

"At the heart of any company wanting to use the Internet to be agile you need these sorts of server technologies," he claims. But he admits that having tangible evidence of product quality isn't enough. What lags behind is the perception that Microsoft can play in this big corporate league. "So we are working as hard as on changing perception and belief as we are on the technology," says Roll.

Next comes the consumer and device division, with the big event here being the 2002 launch of Microsoft's Xbox, another radical departure for the company. Finally, there is the embryonic sector called '.net' (DotNet) which embraces the company's vision for where technology will go in terms of web services. All this comes under the umbrella of the company's professed vision of empowering people through great software any time, any place and on any device.

Perhaps the biggest change is that the company is beginning to realise that reputation matters. According to Roll, "The attributes that we would like people to ascribe to Microsoft include innovation, technology, leadership, vision, and being a responsible leader, both in the community and in the way we do business. If you look at how people think of us now, we are perceived as innovative, as technology leaders, as visionary. But I think we have some way to go in the role we need to take in terms of responsible leadership."

A big part of that is changing the global/local balance to ensure consistency around the world, with a clearer outline of roles and responsibilities. So the headquarters in the US, through a new global advertising council, is putting massive resources behind two centrally developed advertising campaigns: one running now for XP (November 2001) and one starting in January that will be aimed at businesses. That will be co-ordinated with marketing at country level, which has been tightened up considerably.

From a UK viewpoint Roll recalls: "Although we had some very exciting tactical things happening, we didn't do the big things very well. We didn't stand for anything. We were also being inefficient with quite a lot of overlap. So a customer could receive a mailshot from one team one day and another one from another team the next day, with either similar content or mixed messages.

Breaking down autonomous silos is never easy of course. So Roll has designed a structure to promote what he calls connected marketing throughout his 100-strong team. What does that mean in practice? "It means that none of the groups we have created can work in isolation," says Roll. "Culturally it's a big change in the way we market and it is very much for the better, although it will take us time to get there. But the previous silo approach meant that customers weren't getting what they should, that we were being inefficient and we weren't using our resources well."

There are several levels to the new UK marketing organisation, which is a reflection of what is happening elsewhere in the group. There is a department to handle image and reputation, or what Roll calls creating the right environment for Microsoft to do business in. Then there are the product teams like DotNet, PC

Experience (XP) and Servers (for business). They are responsible for broad awareness and excitement generation among audiences.

Customer segment teams have been set up to focus specifically on enterprises, small- to medium-sized businesses and consumers. Partner marketing does what it says, while marketing excellence is responsible for developing the infrastructure, tools and databases that support best practice marketing.

Take the XP launch: "The approach we've taken is that as an organisation there are some big things we feel should be global and consistent around the world and that we should invest in, says Roll. Hence the high profile global campaign. In the UK, this comes after a TV absence of five years. There will also be a range of marketing activities on the ground.

But there's work to be done on a much broader front in terms of reputation. "I look at this in two ways," says Roll. "One is from a technology perspective and the second is from the community perspective." The technology one is complicated. Microsoft has enjoyed a virtual monopoly of desktop operating systems for more than a decade, with 90% share. But now it is confronting Linux, an operating system developed by a Finn, where the code is available to anyone for free.

While it has gained more publicity than actual sales, nevertheless this 'open source' movement has generated a lot of interest – as Roll agrees: "Partly the issue is that people are just glad to have something else." But Microsoft is fighting back with what it calls 'shared source', where the company is making its source code for Windows more visible, to enable developers to share ideas but with Microsoft retaining the intellectual property rights.

There is also an emphasis on community initiatives. In the UK, the company is allied to a number of charities like the National Society for the Prevention of Cruelty to Children and Age Concern, while Microsoft donated over $200 million worth of software to more than 5,000 non-profit organisations around the world.

Above all, Microsoft wants to prove it is indeed listening. This is harder than it sounds. Apart from straddling both consumer and business marketing, there are 40,000 partners in the UK alone who have to be part of the brand positioning. This ranges from retailers, direct marketing agencies and resellers to big strategic integrators, although the 80/20 rule applies: the majority of revenue comes from the top 200.

Roll agrees that consistency can never be guaranteed, but has a programme of marketing activities in place to gain what he calls 'mind share' by exciting partners about what technology can do for their customers. Partner satisfaction is in fact one of the key metrics. Microsoft has developed a measure called CPL – customer/partner loyalty. This is tracked as a priority along with revenue, image and reputation and employee satisfaction. Roll sits on the newly formed global marketing leadership team.

He doesn't minimise the challenge Microsoft faces: "We need to show more and more the business value to an organisation of software, and the exciting things it can do for consumers. And it's much more than marketing because brand isn't something you add on. It has to be inherent in everything we do, from the way we deal with customers to answering the phone."

Changing perception won't be easy to achieve. And new competition is springing up all the time. But going by its track record, it would be dangerous to bet against the company just yet.

Source: *Marketing Business*, November 2001.

Questions

1. What evidence is there in the Case Study that Microsoft is a global thinker?

2. How has it structured the company to operate as a global organisation?

SUMMARY OF KEY POINTS

- The key characteristics of a learning organisation are that they are able to use internal and external feedback to be proactive in adapting to relevant environmental challenges – they are capable of continuous learning and transformation.

- People in learning organisations develop skills that support creativity and innovation within the organisation.

- People in learning organisations are capable of dealing with complex issues and making complex decisions.

- Transnational organisations need to harness creativity and innovation to help them cope with the fragmented and complex business world in which they exist.

- The structure and culture of transnational organisations must enable them to think multinationally but act locally!

- There are many decisions to be made about how to staff overseas business units, including what percentage of national and local staff to use.

- Employees working abroad require considerable support for themselves and their families, so people issues must be tackled at the planning stage.

Improving and developing own learning

The following projects are designed to help you develop your knowledge and skills further by carrying out some research yourself. Feedback is not provided for this type of learning because there are no 'answers' to be found, but you may wish to discuss your findings with colleagues and fellow students.

Project A

By now you will be aware of the importance of giving attention to the people issues when drawing up international marketing plans. Reread Doole & Lowe, *International Marketing Strategy*, 3rd Edition, Chapter 5, pages 167-175 and then review the plan you developed at the end of Session 6 (Projects A, B & C) to make sure you have the right structure within the organisation to enable the people to implement the plan effectively.

What changes might you now make to your plan?

Project B

Read Paliwoda and Thomas, *International Marketing*, 3rd Edition, Chapter 4, Exhibit 4.5: Marketing to Victory.

Why do you think that the restaurant chain has been so successful? What are the advantages of franchising?

Project C

Read Paliwoda and Thomas, *International Marketing*, 3rd Edition, Chapter 9, Exhibit 9.2: Fighting for foreign friends. This discusses how development agencies encourage inward investment.

How effectively are the needs of the people of the organisation considered as part of this process?

Feedback to activities

Activity 7.1

Often the most obvious areas to review are:

- The degree to which the firm carries out a post-evaluation of its programmes and investment decisions positively or constructively – or is there a 'blame' culture?

- Whether real thought is given to periodic re-evaluation of its strategy.

- Whether individuals are encouraged to learn and act more creatively.

Activity 7.2

The organisation structure evolves as the business grows and so must be revised from time to time. Usually decisions are made on the basis of developing senior managers' power bases, on the resources they command or revenue their unit generates. However, some businesses use the structure to demonstrate their commitment to a market-led approach. You will have read two examples of this in the recommended reading for Session 6, Doole & Lowe, *International Marketing Strategy*, 3rd Edition, Chapter 5:

- Illustration 5.3: ABB – a new model of global entrepreneurialism (page 153).

- Illustration 5.6: Unilever prospering through market development (page 172).

Activity 7.3

The key to effective international marketing management is to understand people, their needs and motivations. This applies to all stakeholder relationships but whilst organisations do analyse their customers in-depth, in terms of their people, many focus on:

- The advantages for their managers' career development if they take an overseas post, and

- How much easier it will be to communicate with managers they know;

but fail to consider:

- The additional challenges, problems and disruption facing their own managers when they are working in distant locations; and

- The often demotivating effect it has on local staff.

Session 8

Thinking globally

Introduction

Thinking globally and acting locally has many implied conflicts for organisations that wish to standardise processes and procedures. Therefore generating global strategies is a complex and difficult task. Some of the main considerations and approaches are discussed in this Session.

LEARNING OUTCOMES

At the end of this Session you will be able to:

- Discuss the globalisation process – partnering, alliances and mergers – and their effect on the structure of industry and the competition.

- Discuss the cross-cultural dimensions of global activity and cultural sensitivity.

- Explain the effect of market/economic transience on global operations and within the host country environment.

- Discuss standardisation and differentiation as issues of globalisation.

Alternative views of globalisation

To different people globalisation means different things. To some it is the ultimate threat – the very epitome of corporate greed and arrogance, and the reason for the decline of minority communities and cultures. To others it is the great opportunity to communicate and trade with anyone anywhere in the globe and the way to better understanding and prosperity for more people. What is your view?

There are no entirely satisfactory definitions of globalisation but it is possible to identify a number of drivers of the process of globalisation. Many industries have been changed dramatically by, for example, the opportunity to enter and source components from previously inaccessible markets, to exploit deregulated markets such as financial services and to compete in industries dominated by state owned organisations, such as utilities.

Moves towards common customer requirements have led to the same or similar products being increasingly offered around the world, made to the same industry standards and using the same technology. These trends have provided major new opportunities for growth for some of the largest companies (for example, Sony and Heineken) as well as the most effective niche players, for example high fashion brands.

At the height of the technology revolution in 2000, Vodafone was Europe's largest company and yet it was only established in 1982 as a subsidiary of Racal Electronics. Its growth has been driven by the common global customer need for mobile communications, partly driven by fashion, and the industry's need for transnational technology standards. Vodafone responded to the market needs by a series of business partnerships, joint ventures and takeovers to establish its position but this has not been without risk. The company and license acquisition to run its new services were extremely costly and the market cooled down, leading in 2002 to Vodafone announcing the largest pre-tax loss in history by a UK business of £13.5 billion.

Improved global communications have meant that consumers are aware of the latest news, trends and fashions almost instantly. Designer fashion brands such as Levi Stauss, although niche operators within the textile market, are now huge global companies.

Achieving global reach

However, successfully exploiting these global opportunities and achieving a truly global reach requires financial resources beyond the scope of just about all companies. This has led many firms to adopt specific strategies to extend their power, influence and reach in the many markets around the world. Some firms accept that it may be inappropriate or unnecessary to have global presence (a wholly owned presence in each market) but they still wish to achieve global reach (so their customers can obtain their products or services in all markets). To this end companies pursue co-operative or partnership strategies, either through mergers or joint ventures; or looser arrangements, such as alliances.

Increasingly, more and more of the components and services being used by large firms are being outsourced, to the extent that rather than one firm competing against another, it is one supply chain competing against another. Of course, a major global brand will lead the product or service supply chain, but what percentage of the value of a major brand comes from the firm and what percentage from its suppliers? Alliances and joint ventures might be used for a variety of reasons, such as research and development or joint sales activity, which might be hugely expensive to undertake alone. The result of this is that frequently, two firms might be competing with each other in one product category and co-operating with each other in another.

The arguments for and against globalisation strategies have for the very largest firms, such as Ford, Unilever, Glaxo SmithKline and Sony, become of secondary importance to the need to maximise the benefits from their marketing effort by 'thinking global but acting local'. Such firms as these are determined to enter less developed and emerging markets, despite them being potentially more risky and more difficult to succeed in, because they offer more attractive growth prospects than developed countries and are, therefore, investments for the future.

Whilst these firms would like to use very simple strategies and standardised marketing processes and programmes in the global strategy, in practice they have to adopt a complex combination of strategies – transnational strategies – that can:

- Maximise economies of scale.

- Be adapted to local needs.

- Effectively apply the lessons of good practice that are learned in their SBUs around the world.

Activity 8.1

Carry out an analysis of the trends towards globalisation in your industry sector by considering factors that are part of the process of globalisation, how companies have responded to the factors, and giving examples of company changes, acquisitions and mergers that have been used to implement this response. Fill in the following table using bullet points.

Factors in the process. Globalisation of...	The industry's strategic response to these factors.	Examples of mergers, takeovers and alliances and company changes that have supported this response.
Market access		
Market opportunities		

Factors in the process. Globalisation of...	The industry's strategic response to these factors.	Examples of mergers, takeovers and alliances and company changes that have supported this response.
Industry standards		
Sourcing		
Technology		
Customer requirements		
Competition		
Co-operation		
Distribution		
Communication		

The dimensions of global activity

The trend towards globalisation is a major factor for multinationals and smaller firms and the strategies they adopt. For MNEs a worldwide strategy does not necessarily lead to globally standardised marketing but could mean developing a separate strategy for each international market. The strategy adopted may be:

- **Ethnocentric**, where international operations are seen as secondary to domestic operations. The implications of this are that little attempt is made to understand or modify the marketing mix to suit the needs of the customers in international markets. This is often the approach of exporters and early stage e-marketers.

- **Polycentric**, where independent SBUs are responsible for their own territory (country or region) and develop a marketing strategy to meet the country requirements. This is often referred to as a multi-domestic strategy.

- **Geocentric**, where the organisation views the world as one market, standardising its strategy and marketing mix as far as possible and modifying relatively minor parts of its mix to meet local needs. This is normally viewed as a global strategy.

Transnational strategies are a combination of these strategies.

Cultural sensitivity

The choice of which strategy to use should be based on the firm's competitive advantage and the likely response of the customer base to the products and services offered to exploit this competitive advantage. The major determinant of this is the dimension of culture, which was explored in Session 4. An important development is that of identifying cross-cultural segments that cut across country boundaries. A good example of this is the strategy adopted by Jollibee in the Philippines to compete with McDonald's (which is used in Activity 8.2).

McDonald's identified a segment of the customers that will respond to their existing customer benefits. However, Jollibee identified a significant sub-segment in Asia that want not only fast, reliable food in a clean, pleasant, lively environment, but who also prefer spicy rather than mild tasting food. McDonald's was slow to respond to this and it is clear that Jollibee has gained a competitive edge. Jollibee is set to grow further by offering its version of fast food wherever customers have similar tastes.

This example of the changing basis of competitive advantage in response to greater cultural sensitivity and the demands of customers is mirrored in many other industries. Car buyers around the world who were won over by the reliability and durability of Japanese cars in the 1970s and 1980s became bored and have sought more stylish and innovative cars in the 1990s and 2000s. Similarly customers turned away from previous fashion staples such as blue jeans and white trainers. As a result the fortunes of firms such as Nissan, Levi and Nike took a significant short-term fall.

The key to success for global companies is to ensure that their global brand is perceived positively and is positioned clearly so that the firm's products and services are relevant to buyers from different cultures. This means that there is an increasing need for firms not only to market appropriately developed products but also to design and promote in a culturally sensitive way. There are many examples of firms such as Nike that have used designs and advertising that have offended particular cultures, where the companies have been forced to apologise and withdraw products and advertising.

Activity 8.2

Read the 'Special Focus' feature, *Jollibee, Japan, Johannesburger and Fries* in Doole & Lowe, 2001, International Marketing Strategy, 3rd Edition, pages 279-282 and answer the following questions:

1. What do you consider to be the basis of McDonald's competitive advantage and thus its Unique Selling Propositions (USPs)?

2. What do you consider to be Jollibee's USPs?

3. What aspects of their marketing should (a) McDonald's and (b) Jollibee standardise?

The factors affecting small company operations

The way in which firms organise their global operations is influenced not only by the macro global changes taking place but also by the individual country market and economic environment factors. Their strategies are also influenced by domestic country environment factors.

For smaller firms, internationalisation is typically concerned with entering new markets and modifying products to meet the needs of these markets. There are a number of factors that encourage the firm to internationalise. For example, the firm might build on its success in the home market, or internationalise because of a saturated home market.

Global competition also leads to an increase in the number of foreign competitors attacking the firm in its domestic market. Organisations may be forced to internationalise to survive, but the determinants of success in international markets are likely to be its capability, willingness and ambition to exploit its international opportunities. Whilst exporting is the most obvious market spreading approach, the internationalisation of smaller companies can take a variety of forms.

Some organisations, especially in high technology markets, need to be 'born global' because they must compete worldwide as soon as they are established!

The impact of large company global operations

As a company moves to become more global it places less emphasis on its individual country market and operations. As indicated earlier, establishing a cost-effective supply chain is the key to success for many firms. This means sourcing components and services from the lowest cost supplier and, over time, leads to companies moving their outsourcing or production to ever lower cost countries. As production costs increase in developed countries, so the firm will move its operations to less developed or emerging countries.

However, the decision to close factories is sometimes made not on the basis of factory efficiency but rather on the difficulty of overcoming local laws covering workers' rights. In less developed or emerging markets governments are less able to impose laws to stop firms leaving easily and so inward investment, particularly in setting up service centres, assembly and low added value manufacturing may be short lived. This issue is explored in the Case Study at the end of Session 6. As the economy of the country develops and wages rise, so the operations are moved out and the community is left to try to adjust. Withdrawal of significant investors can have a very detrimental effect on the local economy.

Large firm inward investment can be beneficial, however, if it leads to the creation and development of supply chains within the host country that benefit local manufacture. Also, if the investment is backed with research and development then intellectual property is established in the host country and higher level skills are developed in the local staff. Many emerging countries such as in Central and Eastern Europe have high level engineering skills already but often lack marketing, financial and production management competence.

Activity 8.3

Using the web sites of your government, local authority and inward investment organisation, find out the policy(ies) that is being adopted to encourage investment into your local region or country.

The argument for standardisation

One of the perceptions of globalisation is that it is closely linked with standardisation, i.e. products being exactly the same everywhere in the world. At the outset it is worthwhile recognising that some products (such as computers) are not particularly sensitive to cultural, legal or usage differences, although they may need to be adapted for use (keyboard, instruction manual etc.). Other products, such as food, drinks, retailing and medical treatments may be much more culturally sensitive.

The issue of standardisation has absorbed many writers, such as Ohmae and Levitt, over the last two decades but the truly globally standardised brand or product – a highly desirable objective for some firms – is still rare.

Standardisation gives the potential benefits of economies of scale and the effects of the experience curve – the more times you carry out the same task the more efficiently you do it. But the disadvantage of supplying products that are standardised is that they may not be acceptable for legal reasons or they may not have local appeal and sales revenue will be limited. Often the question facing companies is whether it is better to standardise and attempt to 'educate' consumers to accept the new product or whether it is better to supply an equivalent to the traditional local product.

Companies can enter a new market by:

- Selling their standard product.

- Modifying their product to meet the market needs.

- Developing a new product for the market.

In practice, however, there is a move to standardise the core elements of the total product offer and adapt other elements. So, for example, the Volkswagen group is basing its VW, Audi, Seat and Skoda model range as far as possible on just four 'platforms' whilst modifying the styling to suit market needs.

Standardisation-adaptation continuum

Standardisation, however, goes far beyond just the product P of the marketing mix. The SLEPT factors make it necessary to adapt the mix from market to market. Some elements of international marketing are relatively easy to standardise, whilst others are more difficult. For example, prices are affected by the economics of the country, ability to pay, existing distribution channel options, the country infrastructure and existing market structure. Even achieving uniform positioning of a product or service is extremely difficult, as countries are at different stages of economic development. This means that a product may be an everyday purchase in one country and a luxury in another. Concern for the environment, the perceived importance and different expectations of service and personal aspirations vary considerably from country to country and may be a poor basis on which to build positioning.

In practice, the decision is not whether or not to standardise, but rather where on the standardisation continuum each element of the product offer should be placed.

It may be, therefore, that instead of standardised marketing programmes – such as a pan-regional launch or advertising campaign – the organisation should seek to standardise its worldwide or regional marketing processes – such as marketing research or planning process. It can thus benefit from economies of scale and the experience curve effect, whilst still significantly adapting the components of the process.

Activity 8.4

Evaluation of the organisation's international strategy:

- Does your organisation, no matter how large, have a clear international strategy? What type of generic international strategy has your organisation adopted/should it adopt?

- What is the core proposition for the business that gives it competitive advantage internationally (e.g. good contacts, unique product, high levels of service)? Is it consistent in all markets?

- Where would you place the main elements of the organisation's international marketing strategy on the continuum below?

Completely standardised	Partly standardised	Partly adapted	Completely adapted

---

Case Study – Europe's attitude to the Net

A new survey into European businesses and the Internet and e-commerce has revealed a big divide in attitudes. The survey, which was carried out across seven countries by Datamonitor on behalf of Peoplesoft, asked respondents whether they perceived e-commerce to be a revenue earning tool or a cost saving function.

Sixty eight per cent said that they saw it as a way for their organisations to save money, suggesting that many companies are not fully realising the potential of the Net or, figuring Internet technologies and strategies in their business development plans.

There was a significant difference in the responses when analysed by country: Germany (84%), Sweden (84%) and the Netherlands (77%) in particular, said that they see e-commerce only as a cost saving function.

With 52% of UK respondents saying that they regarded e-commerce as a revenue-generating tool, it seems that the UK is the European country which has most readily accepted the Internet and integrated it most effectively into business models.

The survey also looked at issues of trust and security surrounding the Internet, with a significant number (41%) claiming that they would not use the Internet for large volume transactions and payments. Respondents from Sweden and France seemed the most confident in the Internet's security, with 75% and 72% respectively saying they would use the Internet for large financial transactions.

Financial services is the business sector leading the way in Internet acceptance, 69% saying they had no problem with conducting large payments online and only 56% saying they saw the Internet as merely a cost saving function.

Source: *Marketing Business*, October 2000.

Questions

1. If national culture is reflected in organisational attitudes, what are the implications for international marketers of different attitudes to the Internet in different countries?

2. What impact would increasing consumer confidence in security for financial transactions on the Internet have on global reach for international companies?

SUMMARY OF KEY POINTS

- Having a global presence is very important to many large companies who need to be seen expanding operations successfully across the world.

- Global organisations need to develop strategies that allow them to employ the advantages of economy of scale but still be adaptable to local circumstances and needs.

- Culture plays an important role in helping organisations define what is acceptable locally from their global offerings.

- Separate national strategies may be ethnocentric, polycentric or geocentric.

- Smaller companies may select exporting as their international market entry method because it is less complex and often represents a lower risk factor than other methods. However, competition and the nature of the industry may lead them to consider other means of entry.

- Standardisation is a big issue for all organisations and each element of the marketing mix should be considered separately, rather than a blanket policy of standardisation being adopted.

Improving and developing own learning

The following projects are designed to help you develop your knowledge and skills further by carrying out some research yourself. Feedback is not provided for this type of learning because there are no 'answers' to be found, but you may wish to discuss your findings with colleagues and fellow students.

Project A

Visit the web sites of organisations such as Ford, Unilever, Glaxo SmithKline and Sony to find out what strategies they are adopting to enter less developed and emerging markets.

Project B

For a product of your choice, consider the issues involved in introducing it to consumers in a less developed country.

Use the Internet to research the market in the country of your choice.

Project C

When marketing across borders it is often more difficult to standardise price and distribution than product and sales promotion. Examine one or more of the products or services that your organisation produces, or products of your choice, and select a country to introduce them to.

What aspects can be standardised and what would need to be fully customised for the 'local' market?

Feedback to activities

Activity 8.1

We have included below some examples from the mobile telephone industry to get you started:

Factors in the process. Globalisation of...	The industry's strategic response to these factors.	Examples of mergers, takeovers and alliances and company changes that have supported this response.
Market access	China is an important target market because it offers huge potential, because of the small number of fixed telephone lines.	Global mobile phone operators have taken stakes in existing companies in emerging markets to enable them to gain a foothold.

Market opportunities	Deregulation of government owned telephone companies has provided opportunities for new players.	In the UK the new mobile phone operators have grown fast whereas previously state-owned BT has struggled to respond fast enough to the changes.
Sourcing	Common standards and global companies provide.	Nokia re-invented itself to be a mobile phone supplier and has grown very fast indeed.
Co-operation	The challenge is to create global networks for the benefit of travellers.	Many examples such as Vodafone-Mannesman merger.

Activity 8.2

1. The issue here is for McDonald's to define more clearly their segmentation basis as sub-segments are appearing in the global fast food market and some difficult decisions must be made in defining the target segments and positioning. It is no longer possible to be 'all things to everyone'.

2. Jollibee have developed a more focused cross-cultural Segmentation, Targeting and Positioning (STP) strategy and can now offer products to their defined fast food segment that add value – by being adapted to the taste of that cross-cultural segment.

3. If you have defined the strategy for the two companies in your answers for 1 and 2, you should be able to decide what can be standardised from the standardisation-adaptation continuum shown on Doole & Lowe, page 225.

Activity 8.3

From the pattern that emerges it should be possible to:

■ Determine the industry sectors being attracted.

■ Identify any links between your country and the country of the inward investor that are being exploited.

- Decide what selling propositions for your country or region are being used.

- Decide whether the investment being attracted will be sustainable.

Activity 8.4

The main issues to consider are:

- Whether the strategy is clear, understandable and appropriate in the current situation and whether it is being pursued by all parts of the organisation.

- Inconsistency in different situations and countries may be defended by the local managers but may lead to internal conflicts.

- You might wish to think about the changes in the placing of the elements on the continuum over the last two years. Are you moving towards greater standardisation and is this delivering additional benefits?

Session 9

Entry strategies

Introduction

This Session examines how organisations use all the information gathered on the international market they wish to enter, and make decisions on appropriate strategies for market entry.

LEARNING OUTCOMES

At the end of this Session you will be able to:

- Discuss the different strategies available to companies for market entry and development.

- Explain the criteria to use when identifying and selecting an appropriate strategy for market entry.

- Explain how companies can obtain finance to support market entry.

Market entry options

Market entry options include:

- Exporting.

- Multi-national sales force.

- International distributors.

- Franchising.

- Licensing.

- Joint venture.

- Acquisition.

- Fully owned, operational subsidiary.

The options outlined above, and additional ones detailed in the recommended reading for this Session, span a level of international involvement by a company from virtually zero – when the firm merely makes the products available for others to export but effectively does nothing itself to market its products internationally –

to businesses in which only a small proportion of their income is generated in the domestic market.

The large number of possible market entry strategies can be put into four categories: indirect exporting, direct exporting, foreign manufacturing strategies and co-operation strategies.

- **Indirect exporting** methods are attractive to companies which have little inclination or few resources for international marketing. It offers them a simple and low-cost method of market entry which gives them access to international markets by having their products sold internationally by others. Whilst indirect exporting has the advantage of the least cost and risk of any entry method, it allows the company little control over how, when, where and by whom the products are sold. In some cases, the domestic company may even be unaware that its products are being exported.

- **Direct exporting** gives a company benefits of direct over indirect exporting in that the proactive approach makes it easier to exert more influence over international activities. This results in a number of specific advantages for the exporter such as greater control over the selection of market and elements of the marketing mix, improved feedback about the performance of individual products and the opportunity to build up expertise in international marketing.

  The disadvantages of direct exporting are that the direct investment necessary is considerable because the whole of the marketing, distribution and administration costs will now be borne by the company. In taking this decision, the company must be quite sure that the costs can be justified in the light of the market opportunities identified.

- **Foreign manufacture** can involve a high level of risk. However, at some point in its international development, a stage is reached when the pressure increases upon a company to make a much more substantial commitment to an individual market or region. There can be many reasons for investment in local operations; perhaps to gain new business or defend existing business, to save costs or simply avoid government restrictions. A move into foreign manufacture involves high cost and risk. However, firms can choose between different levels of financial commitment depending on whether they decide to simply set up an assembly or licensing operation, acquire an existing business or the most costly option of all, set up a greenfield site.

- **Co-operation strategies** tend to be one of two kinds; a joint venture which is usually an equity based venture, or a strategic alliance. Whilst all market entry methods essentially involve alliances of some kind, the term strategic alliance is used to cover a variety of contractual arrangements which are intended to be strategically beneficial to both parties and which cannot be defined as clearly as licensing or joint ventures. In strategic alliances at least two companies combine value chain activities for the purpose of competitive advantage. Perhaps one of the most significant aspects of strategic alliances has been that it has frequently involved co-operation between partners who might in other circumstances be competitors.

These four categories vary significantly in terms of levels of control they offer a company and the level of risk involved. The cost of resourcing the alternative methods usually equates closely to levels of involvement and risk. Often associated with higher levels of involvement is not only greater potential for control, but also higher potential risk, usually due to the high cost of investment. Thus, when considering the different strategies available for market entry and development, a company must review the implications of the various options in terms of:

- The level of control over the international business that it requires.

- The level of risk it is willing to take.

- What resources are available to the company, now and in the future.

Activity 9.1

For a company of your choice:

1. Outline the main market entry methods the company uses in its global markets.

2. Specify the key advantages and disadvantages of each of the strategies to the company.

Selection criteria

The criteria that a company may use to evaluate which of the options discussed in the previous section is most appropriate, may vary depending on the outlook of the company and the objectives it wishes to achieve on its international markets.

Companies sometimes tend to approach involvement in international markets rather cautiously, and there is an underlying life cycle with critical success factors which change as a firm moves along the various stages of international development. For the small and medium-sized firms, their activity in international markets may only ever develop as far as exporting and so effectively close off many of the options discussed. Exporting may well remain the best option for these types of companies if they lack both the resources and the commitment to get involved in other forms of international business.

The criteria perceived as important may depend on the size of the company and the level of involvement in international markets it wishes to achieve. The culture of the country where the company is based may also influence the criteria used in selecting an appropriate market entry strategy. Japanese companies tend to have a highly globalised perspective on international markets and develop subsidiaries around the world to deliver their core market entry strategy. By contrast, German companies are seen as being much more cautious in their international involvement, preferring to invest in German companies inside Germany itself, and develop direct exporting strategies.

It is important to emphasise the risk assessment that any firm makes when considering different market entry options. The company will be concerned with such criteria as market situation, company objectives and competitor activity and also how the entry selection might be made against the background of the need to reduce risks and improve the chances of success. For a lot of companies as discussed earlier, exporting in some form is the automatic choice, but for larger firms all the entry options identified may be possible choices.

Challenges for small and large companies

For a small business, the selection of a suitable market entry method is about entering new markets in a cost effective way, but the challenges to a manager are to manage the risk and avoid making arrangements which might adversely affect the firm's long-term objectives. This demands an understanding of each new market and a vision of how each might develop.

The effectiveness of a firm's exporting activity depends to a considerable degree on management attitudes and commitment, and some very small but very dynamic businesses achieve high sales levels by exporting. Developing an international perspective in the very early days may increasingly become a characteristic of a successful business.

Managers of larger firms face the challenge of making new entry decisions against a background of an existing network of international operations. Critical to this are decisions on timing and sequence. The management of different entry methods in different countries presents particular problems if the objective is to maintain a consistent approach across international markets. Whilst this is a major problem for multinationals, it is equally difficult for a small business to manage image and quality through an overseas license or franchise across a number of markets.

Multinationals have the problem of managing their levels of involvement in substantially different market situations. Often this leads to the need to make decisions about whether they should co-operate or compete with other companies. Rarely can market entry be achieved by a company operating alone. Most involve relationships with other individuals or companies and it is these relationships which are usually central to the success of the entry strategy.

The selection of the entry method is vitally important in ensuring that products and services have the right image and level of exposure in each market. Selecting an entry method with little direct commitment to the market sends confusing and often negative messages to the market; for example, lack of availability of products, the image of products made overseas or high prices because of a long supply chain. A joint venture or strategic alliance, if not managed well, may also present confused branding to consumers.

Sometimes companies use a low risk entry strategy to gain a hold in a market but then find they need a much higher level of involvement if they are to progress in the market. Xerox had a distributor in Japan for many years but failed to develop what they saw as their potential in the market. They then formed a joint venture with Fuji to directly involve themselves in the market and so gain more control as well as access to the latest technical developments. Likewise in the telecommunications industry Motorola and Fujitsu have recently formed a joint venture and in Italy Vodafone have developed an alliance with Omnitel in order to enter that market.

The choice of an appropriate market entry method has a crucial role in enabling the firm to meet its objectives, solve particular problems and exploit opportunities.

Activity 9.2

For the company you identified in Activity 9.1, specify what you think are the important criteria the company should consider in deciding an appropriate market entry strategy.

Financing market entry

The international marketing manager increasingly needs to be knowledgeable about the various complexities of financing international marketing transactions and sources of finance to support marketing entry. Traditionally, to support market entry strategies managers seek financial support through commercial banks, government sponsored loans or some kind of co-operation agreement.

Commercial banks compete intensively to offer international trade services to companies operating in different countries. However they tend only to be willing to support low-risk activities, which sometimes makes it difficult for companies expanding into emerging markets to obtain finance to support market entry.

Commercial banks may also be more interested in short-term financing. This potentially makes them not such a good source for companies making long-term investment decisions in incipient markets, because it may be several years before a full return on investment can be achieved. Many banks which made long-term loans to developing markets have suffered losses when countries not experiencing the growth rates expected have been unable to meet debt repayments. This has led to a number of banks being less willing to expose themselves in long-term, high-risk markets.

This has led to companies which operate in international markets to seek other forms of financing to support market entry. One such way is **forfeiting**. This is a way of financing without recourse. This means that companies selling products essentially transfer the transaction risk to a forfeiting house. A bill of exchange is drawn up to the value of the contract and the seller transfers the claim resulting from the transaction to the forfeiting house. The seller immediately receives the full amount of the contract minus the discount agreed for the period of the contract. This discount will vary depending on the length of the contract, the level of country risk and whether the invoice is guaranteed by a commercial bank. For the company it provides a source of finance to support medium-term contracts in a market and provides a means of reducing the risk of non-payment.

Some organisations may qualify for government-sponsored finance. The ability to assemble a good financial package may well determine the competitive advantage of a company in trying to develop marketing entry strategies. For this reason governments are often willing to support companies financially because they realise that such financial support may lead to economic growth in the home country and boost employment. National governments approach such support in a variety of ways. In most countries there is an export-import bank or perhaps an export bank or, as in the UK, a government department (Trade Partners UK) who fund a variety of support packages to encourage firms to export and to help those who are exporting to finance longer-term export strategies.

Co-operation agreements are special kinds of counter-trade deals that extend over long periods of time and may have government involvement. They may be called product purchase transactions, buyback deals or pay as you earn deals. For example, a company may obtain finance to help set up a factory in a particular country if they then agree to buy back the output of the plant. The Swedish company Ikea leased machinery and equipment to a plant in Poland to upgrade production in exchange for an export contract.

Counter-trade deals are more prevalent when companies are trying to enter emerging or less developed markets and not so common in highly developed markets. The reasons for this are threefold:

- It is sometimes difficult to obtain finance commercially to enter such markets.

- The markets themselves may have limited access to hard currency, which means the finance of joint ventures or strategic alliances has to be sought through less traditional means.

- Emerging markets may see such deals as a way of encouraging job creation in their own countries and so actively encourage such financing deals.

Activity 9.3

Prepare a short report for your company management on the various services the bank most closely related to your company offers which would help your company finance its international market entry strategies.

Which ones do you think are most relevant to your company?

Case Study – Let the battle commence

Britain's Post Office (PO) is getting irritated. The EC commission has poured cold water on its plans for a leisurely move towards liberalisation and instead issued a draft directive, which is likely to lead to a scramble for power among Europe's major domestic operators.

The announcement from the department headed by Dutchman Frits Bolkestein, which is responsible for regulating the £53bn postal sector, stated three key aims:

to reduce the letters monopoly to 50g; to liberalise direct mail; and to liberalise outbound, but not incoming, cross border mail.

This is much too soon, claims the PO. "The Commission are taking a leap of faith", says its chief executive, John Roberts. "They are going far too quickly. The proposals run the risk of damaging postal services throughout the EU and the losers will be customers everywhere in the EC."

Oh yes? Or is it just that the PO would have liked longer to consolidate its role in the international arena before competitors make too many inroads into the UK? David Robottom, the Direct Marketing Association's (DMA) director of development and postal affairs, pulls no punches.

"The big issue is whether overseas acquisition being made by these operators come from monopoly profits they have made in their own markets," he says. "We have written to the Commissioner on this. We don't mind the PO building an international network but where is the money coming from?

"The DMA has supported the PO in its aim of being the best postal service in the world but it should sort out its domestic marketplace first. There is investment needed in the UK network. They have reorganised, but not made any progress."

Empire building, however, appears to be the name of the game, with three European operators leading the chase: the British PO (which incorporates Royal Mail), Germany's Deutsche Post and TNT Post Group (TGP) of the Netherlands. In fact the PO and TGP have even formed a joint venture with Singapore's postal operator in international mail.

Viewed from the outside there appear to be differences in approach between the Royal Mail and Deutsche Post brands. "From past experience with both companies," says Alexandra Uhlmann, director of the brand development programme at Ashbridge Management College, "I think Royal Mail is investing much more in below-the-line advertising, not positioning itself with consumers, but loyalty building. Deutsche Post, by contrast, is investing above the line, most noticeably by spending large sums of money recently on its sponsorship of the Formula One Jordan team with Benson & Hedges. It is trying to be seen as a global player."

In contrast, Royal Mail sponsorships tend to be worthy but often low profile, mostly dedicated to the schools market or b2b. Indeed, its venture into international sponsorship some years back through its involvement with the Olympics appears to have dampened enthusiasm. The result is a strategy that appears somewhat at odds with the company's overall marketing objectives. But Uhlmann appears to be exactly right about Deutsche Post.

"The investment gives the company worldwide measurable attention, which otherwise we would have to pay for via classical PR disciplines," says Donald Brooks, managing director of Deutsche Post Global Mail. "Deutsche Post is associated with positive attributes like reliability and seriousness. However, it still carries the image of a bureaucratic government institution, which we need to change.

"Deutsche Post World Net is indeed one of the largest and most efficient letter and logistics groups in the world. In the year of our IPO, sponsoring F1 gives us the opportunity to show millions of customers and potential investors that Deutsche Post is a quick and competent partner you can trust for logistical solutions worldwide. The main aim is to introduce Deutsche Post on an international platform and to emphasise three particular attributes of the Group: competitiveness, speed and competence – qualities which are also manifested in F1."

The British Post Office, which through Royal Mail is currently spending $10m on a TV campaign telling businesses to listen to their customers, is going to be hard pressed if it chooses to directly oppose Deutsche Post using its advertising budget on an international business. But then, maybe it will choose a different route. For if its CE Roberts is to be believed, customers will vote with their feet because of its performance.

"To compete successfully in a global sector, postal services must become complete distribution companies with global reach," he says. "As income from domestic operations declines, they must become companies that people choose to do business with. This means doing things for the right price and in the right way. Postal services must offer better value for money through improved service and quality and greater cost efficiency.

Both operators obviously have the same objectives; the question is can both achieve it? Deutsche Post, for instance, has been acknowledged recently by the US postal service as the biggest post office in the world through its acquisitions, according to the DMA's Robottom. "I believe that the British PO wants to be in a similar position," he says.

Even though Deutsche Post has cherry picked many of the key companies, inflating the prices of those that are left, the British PO is no slouch in this area. It has spent £500m on overseas acquisitions and joint ventures with more, it promises, to come. It is particularly strong in the global parcels market. As Robottom says, "They haven't caught up with Deutsche Post yet, but they are getting there."

The worry is though, that with all this focus on acquisitions, postal operators have taken their eye off the ball. None seems to have fully taken on board the implications of the Internet. Beleaguered Trade Secretary Stephen Byers did his best, promising giant government subsidies to transform post offices into Internet centres and online focal points for advice on benefits, job vacancies, health and transport.

Yet when a company like the Telegraph Group, one of the UK's most prolific mailers, is reported to be mailing just 25% of its normal quota of questionnaires, relying on other media such as the phone, then postal operators need to take note.

We're likely to see some tough tactics in the UK. "Business users want choice, and since the incumbent has a good reputation, Deutsche Post will have to compete on service, quality, predictability, measurability and price," says Robottom. "Price will have a role but it won't be the be all and end all. Both operations will look to added value. If Deutsche Post brings all those qualities, it stands a good chance. But historically, incumbents, if performing to their best, tend not to lose much market share. Just look at BT."

What each country's post office has to juggle with, however, is the Universal Service Obligation (USO): the guaranteeing of a universal standard of service at a single price, regardless of where consumers live. This was quantified by the National Economic Research Association (NERA) in research commissioned by the EC. Working out a system which pleases all parties, however, is unlikely to be easy.

"The outcome is a difficult balancing act, requiring honest communication about costs between companies and regulators," says Ian Senior, special advisor to NERA. "As for the PO and Deutsche Post, both administrations want to slow the pace of liberalisation in their markets. The British PO has said it is in favour of controlled liberalisation, offering to reduce the minimum price that competitors could charge from £1 to 75p, which would have yielded some of the market. That's on hold at the moment. But they haven't shown signs of wanting to open up the market substantially."

Deutsche Post argues that the effects of liberalisation are unequal. "Distortion of competition will continue even when the guidelines have been implemented in all EU countries," says Brooks. "Thus, in addition to those where there is no exclusive licensing agreement, or where it has been strongly reduced (Sweden, Finland and Germany for example), there will be countries where the monopoly permitted under the EU guidelines is exploited to the full. The requirements with regard to universal service also vary dramatically. We need an even playing field for competition".

In which case Martin Stanley, CE of the Postal Services Commission (Postcomm), could be the answer to his prayers. "We aim to introduce some competition, set a fair but tight control on prices and set challenging but fair standards," he says.

"The PO has a monopoly on below £1 delivery," he says. "Below that it has enormous power given its size. A company of that size can take losses and risks that a smaller company can't. It also has privileges, it gets preferential customer treatment, can park on yellow lines where other companies can't, and it does not get charged VAT – a major advantage. So the playing field does not appear level and we are looking at that."

It is also looking at what customers want for the first time, with a budget of £1.5m to talk to PO customers across all its markets – a first in the postal market at home and abroad. The aim is to have an organisation shaped by customer need.

"But we can only recommend what the government should do, not force our recommendations," says Stanley. "And it may be difficult to get parliamentary time for changes. We can't stop the PO investing where it wants to invest, but we can ensure that it is not on the back of subsidies from the domestic market. And if we think that losses might be subsidised from the profits of domestic mail, we will do our best to stop that. From now on it can't make major international acquisitions without our involvement."

Stanley is enthusiastic about his task: "The aim is to get competition, if we can do so without destroying the universal service. We will be acting as proxy for the customer, aiming to give them a good service." But he is realistic about the dangers. "At the moment the Royal Mail is profitable," he says. "It is cheaper to deliver on some routes than others, so there has to be some cost subsidy. On the other hand, any company charged with providing a national service has to incur some costs. As long as the PO has a monopoly, it is easier to apply the USO. The danger is if there is cherry picking, then there is less ability to cross-subsidise, and this is what we have to guard against. But there is plenty of scope before we reach that stage."

What Stanley proposes is a truly customer-focused organisation, with the Commission setting high service standards and penalising the PO if it doesn't meet them. He understands that, in a monopoly, it makes sense to operate in a way that suits your organisation rather than the customer, but, he says, "We have to bring in a situation where the customer is king." Speaking as a customer whose mail arrives at 1.30pm most days, the time can't come soon enough!

At a glance

■ The EC have issued a draft directive to liberalise the European postal sector.

■ Although the British PO and Deutsche Post have different approaches to their marketing strategies, both are actively expanding their global interests through acquisitions and partnerships.

■ Both companies will need to look at adding value, while abiding by the USO – a guarantee of a universal standard of service.

■ The Postal Services Commission will be making recommendations to the Government as to how to introduce competition that will benefit customers.

Source: *Marketing Business*, September 2000.

Questions

1. What opportunities and threats exist for the British PO?

2. What competitive strategies could the British Post Office employ against Deutsche Post and other competition in the event that their monopoly is broken?

SUMMARY OF KEY POINTS

■ There are many different strategies available to companies for market entry and development, each of which represent a different level of involvement in international marketing.

■ Small firms may select exporting as a suitable means of market entry due to its relatively low risk factor.

■ Large companies generally have the knowledge and experience to use all types of market entry option and their decision may revolve around the level of risk they wish to take, the degree of control they wish to exercise in the market and the cost factors involved.

- Obtaining finance to support market entry depends on the degree of involvement required.

- Most organisations need to develop relationships with other organisations, including those such as banks and government departments willing to sponsor inward investment in order to finance and support market entry.

Improving and developing own learning

The following projects are designed to help you develop your knowledge and skills further by carrying out some research yourself. Feedback is not provided for this type of learning because there are no 'answers' to be found, but you may wish to discuss your findings with colleagues and fellow students.

Project A

Read Paliwoda and Thomas, *International Marketing*, Chapter 4, Exhibit 4.6: Where does your car come from? And Exhibit 4.9: Ford taps into Asia through Mazda.

Use the Internet to search for further articles that indicate the changes that are taking place in the small car manufacturing industry.

Project B

Read Paliwoda and Thomas, *International Marketing*, Chapter 4, Exhibit 4.7: BT pieces together a global jigsaw.

Use the Internet to research how effectively BT has entered the Asia Pacific region since that article was written.

Project C

Read Paliwoda and Thomas, *International Marketing*, Chapter 4, Exhibit 4.11: L'Oreal makes up strategies for emerging markets.

Use the Internet to follow up their progress.

Feedback to activities

Activity 9.1

Market entry decisions are determined mainly by the organisation's business objectives and its attitude to international marketing. In tackling the activity you need therefore firstly to understand these aspects with respect to the company you are examining. The essential differences in market entry methods centre on:

- Cost.
- Potential for return on investment.
- Levels of risk, in terms of finance, image and long-term performance.
- The level of control in its export markets that the company wishes to achieve.

Activity 9.2

This activity is asking you to reflect on the discussions you had when undertaking Activity 9.1 and list the factors that management perceived as important to them in justifying their answers to that question. Were they what you expected? If not, why not?

Activity 9.3

To complete this activity you will need to contact the international trade services department of the bank in order to obtain the necessary information. You may find the information available on the web site of the company's personal bank. In evaluating which are most relevant you need to ascertain:

- The type of markets your company exports to and whether they have a high level of transaction risk.
- The type of customers and the length of time the company has been dealing with them.
- The credit period the company operates.
- The size of the contracts and the time taken for contract completion.

Session 10

Managing products and brands

Introduction

This Session explores the issues relating to product management in international markets. As you will appreciate from previous Sessions, there are additional factors – particularly cultural – that complicate decisions about managing brands across borders and implications for new product development. However, the emergence of so-called 'global brands' indicates that many opportunities exist for the competent global organisation and international marketer.

LEARNING OUTCOMES

At the end of this Session you will be able to:

- Identify product management strategies available to companies.

- Discuss how to select and formulate a product management strategy.

- Discuss image, branding and positioning in international markets.

- Discuss policies and processes for international new product development.

The international product and service offer

The product or service 'offer' is usually central to the international marketing strategy. In this section we refer to product, but in doing so we include services too. Services, such as accountancy, law, travel and healthcare are rapidly growing in importance in international marketing.

You should familiarise yourself with the concept that 'pure' products, and 'pure' services might be considered to be at opposite ends of a continuum, with most product offers including service elements. The product offer consists not just of the core physical properties, but is augmented by additional elements such as packaging, warranties, after sales service and branding that make up the total offer. All these elements must be designed to appeal to the customer. Think about your own organisation's offer in terms of its product elements and service elements.

The service element of a total product offer is becoming an increasingly important differentiator of competitive product offers. In any marketing mix planning you should always think in terms of the 7Ps and include the 3 service Ps (people, physical evidence and process) as well as the more traditional 4Ps. For example, in the business-to-business market a manufacturer of components can no longer produce to a drawing that is supplied by its customer, but rather has to provide design, research and development and technical support services for their product. At the very least, consumers expect frontline staff to have good product knowledge so they can give advice to assist product selection.

The international product strategy choices

The fundamental decision in product management is concerned with the degree to which the product offer can and should be standardised throughout all its markets and the degree to which it must be adapted in its various markets. Even with truly global products such as Coca-Cola and McDonald's, only a few elements of the total offer (typically the corporate identity and image) can be standardised throughout the world. Cultural factors, usage factors, legal standards and product liability can all lead to the need for adaptation of the product to local taste and needs, e.g. sweetness in Coca-Cola or meat content and spiciness in McDonald's.

Firms have a choice regarding their overall international product strategic approach. They can:

- Offer a product that is or has been successful at home and sell it to consumers in a new country without any modification.

- Find out what consumers are buying in a particular market and supply it.

- Design a product that will have appeal to a global customer segment.

Product strategies include the design, production or sourcing and delivery of products and services, and so there are other issues to consider.

The product strategy should also include ethical considerations. Safe products should be offered at a fair price for the consumer. The products should not harm the environment, nor involve the exploitation of people in their development, production or delivery. Organisations must become increasingly sensitive to these issues because of the greater awareness of customers of production conditions and the impact that production has on the surrounding environment and community.

Activity 10.1

Consider the implication of current trends on product policy. What trends are currently affecting the product policies of international organisations? We have identified the first few and you should list others in the left-hand column of the table below. When you have done this you should go back and list the implications for strategy development in the second column of the table.

Trends affecting product policy	Implications for strategy development	
	General	Our industry
Product differentiation.	It is increasingly difficult to differentiate core products and so it is likely to be one or more of the elements of the augmented product and the three Ps that provide the firm with its source of competitive advantage.	
Increased competition from 'own label' products.	Smaller pricing premium for top brands.	
Shorter product life cycles.	Need to reduce the investment pay back cycle – e.g. by using alliances for worldwide distribution.	
Increased counterfeiting.		

Building a product portfolio for international markets

Against the background of factors discussed in the previous section, it is clear that organisations must:

- Select products and services from their product portfolio to meet the needs of a precisely targeted international customer segment; and

- Build the product/service portfolio by retaining, modifying or eliminating existing products and developing new products and services.

With ever-shorter product life cycles and the need to keep the product portfolio fresh, it is necessary to have an effective approach for the introduction and elimination of products. The organisation will place emphasis upon new product development and exploiting new processes and systems whilst at the same time maximising the financial contribution of existing products and services. As indicated earlier, the augmented elements of the product such as packaging, after sales service, and warranties can provide the main point of differentiation and may be the focus for innovation.

Product Life Cycles (PLC)

In thinking about Product Life Cycles (PLC) and international product portfolios, and, for example, the Boston Consulting Group matrix (BCG) you need to consider two dimensions. The company will have a portfolio of products at different stages of the product life cycle with each in different quadrants of the BCG portfolio matrix. However, It is also likely that each individual product is at different stages of the PLC and in different quadrants of the BCG matrix in the different countries in which it is being marketed.

The company is faced with deciding whether to use its resources to accelerate its entry into different country markets with its existing products or to develop new products. This dilemma is further complicated as shorter PLCs and the increasing cost of research and development are forcing businesses to achieve much faster time scales for the development, launch and diffusion of new products throughout their world markets to maintain cash flow and reduce the investment payback period. As a result, it may employ different market entry methods such as joint ventures and strategic alliances and standardised marketing management processes.

For many companies the elimination of products can be a critical decision. Often a product that is performing poorly overall can be a cash cow or star in one or two countries. Eliminating the product can upset loyal customers in those markets.

Competition factors

The competitive situation is a significant factor in determining the company's strategy. Depending on the strength of its portfolio or new product the company might choose:

- To compete head on with its major competitor in the high profile global market.

- To quietly establish a bridgehead into a market where the competitor is weak or the new entrant will not be perceived to be a major threat.

The strategies of recent entrants into the airline business have demonstrated this. Virgin maintained a direct attack on British Airways in the global market fighting to win passengers from BA in the long haul flights, by offering a differentiated service. By contrast, the 'no frills' airlines, such as easyJet and Ryanair, have focused on low price short distance national or regional flights. Initially the larger airlines only saw these no-frills airlines as a small threat in one limited customer segment. However, as passengers now want more frequent low cost flights, the segment has grown rapidly. Southwest Airlines in the US first established in 1967 the 'no frills' approach. In Asia, despite the birth of a number of new small airlines, the market has not yet really developed yet, mainly because the largest cities are quite long distances apart.

A company's geographic development may also depend upon the nature of the industry sector. Some sectors are truly global (for example, aircraft manufacture, computers, luxury products), some are progressing towards being global but have constraints (for example, pharmaceuticals and telecommunications). The core product or service in some cases is common in different markets but requires local adaptation (for example, electrical goods) and finally, other products and services are very specific to their local market (for example, retailing and certain foods).

Activity 10.2

Select a major product category of your organisation, or one you know well, and use the international product life cycle (Doole & Lowe, *International Marketing Strategy*, 3rd Edition, Figure 9.2, page 307) and portfolio analysis matrix (Figure 9.3, page 309) to plot the performance of the product or service in a number of international markets.

- At what stage is the product in its major markets?

- In which of the markets is the product under-performing?

- Should the company focus on market development or product development?

Country of origin

Image, branding and the positioning of a company's products and services are influenced by the marketing activities it undertakes (for example, using the marketing mix) but these are ultimately decided according to the perceptions of the company's customers. Corporate and brand identity are developed by the organisation – image is what the consumer perceives.

The Country of Origin (COO) provides the basis of the first assessment of a product or service offer by a customer. COO affects customer purchasing behaviour because of:

- Preconceived notions about different countries.

- Preconceived notions about the quality of the products they design and make.

These stereotypes then generate in the consumer certain beliefs about both the product and the image of the company that is perceived to originate from that country. For example, Harley Davidson is strongly associated with images of the US.

Branding

There have been a number of attempts to define what a brand is, and perhaps even more attempts to define a global brand. Typical definitions of branding usually make reference to quality, satisfaction and values and it is clear that brand identity is very significant, especially in consumer brands. However, brand image is determined by the perception of its positioning and personality in the marketplace.

Think about how some brands with which you are familiar are positioned differently in different country markets. The greatest brands travel internationally because they have a robust identity with universal appeal. The brand is supported by every action that the company and its staff take, rather than simply being an identity that the company tries to create and associate with the product or service name. Hence it can be damaged or enhanced by action taken by the people of the organisation form the Chief Executive to the delivery driver.

One of the most common mistakes made in brand management is overstretching the brand by using it with products that consumers cannot associate with the brand. Equally, under-use of the brand is also a sign of poor management. Identify some examples of each of these situations in organisations that you are familiar with.

There are a number of reasons for brands declining in value and you might consider which of the following elements explain the difficulties experienced by those you thought of:

- General long term neglect.
- Inappropriate positioning.
- Market decline and failure to reposition.
- Inappropriate brand stretching.
- Failure to stretch the brand.
- Starvation of the brand through lack of promotional support.
- Poor response to new competition.
- Mishandling of sudden and unexpected crises.

One of the most difficult challenges for brand management is dealing with unexpected crises that are almost inevitable from time to time. They can be the result of unexpected events in the environment; for example, the unreasonable or criminal behaviour of disaffected employees, or antisocial individuals or groups. Crises can also occur because of cultural insensitivity or inappropriate actions by the company's staff. Nike has caused offence to religious groups through the inappropriate use of slogans and posters and markings on trainers.

The critical issue is how the crises are dealt with, as this will ultimately determine whether the crisis has a detrimental effect on the brand value. Honest and rapid admission of failure is usually the best policy, followed by recompense if required.

Activity 10.3

Test out your own preconceived ideas about the products from particular countries by completing the following sentences using just one or two words. The important thing is **not to think too much** before you complete the sentence!

German products are ....
French products are ....
Italian products are ....
American products are ....
Japanese products are ....
British products are ....
Russian products are ....
Chinese products are ....

New Product Development (NPD)

In this Companion, we have already discussed a number of the factors that influence the choice of policies and processes of New Product Development (NPD) and their implications. These include:

- The identification of international market segments allows more precise targeting, better design of more globally acceptable new products and faster acceptance.

- The need to be close to consumers to understand their needs: acceptance or need for adaptation of standardised products.

- The shorter PLCs, faster 'copying' and the shorter investment payback times requiring faster and more effective diffusion of the new product throughout the world.

- The higher cost of research and development and the decreasing number of 'new-to-the-world' products and services.

- The increase in mobility of staff and the increase in knowledge transfer make it more difficult to retain intellectual property within the company.

- Improved communication and awareness of the performance of companies.

- The need to pay increasing attention to product liability laws in certain countries, and assess the potential risks and opportunities associated with cultural sensitivity and different usage conditions, particularly in LDCs.

- Improving education in many LDCs, leading to the need to access the best ideas from everywhere.

Some companies are responding to these factors by making decisions about how their Research and Development (R&D) activities should be organised.

Consider the arguments for centralisation or decentralisation of R&D. Decentralised R&D should enable the organisation to obtain a better understanding of local market conditions and to access the best knowledge and ideas from particular 'hotspots', for example universities or clusters of businesses (e.g. Silicon Valley).

Centralisation of R&D, however, should help the organisation to maintain confidentiality of knowledge. The increasing mobility of staff, more frequent industrial espionage as well as the increasing transparency of communications (for example, the Internet) is making it much easier for companies to communicate with their worldwide stakeholders, but at the same time harder for them to hold on to their secrets.

There is an increasing trend towards co-operating on research and development (even between competitors) because of the high costs involved. Companies are becoming much more willing to outsource different elements of the NPD process to niche providers.

A key issue for NPD is the increased speed required when developing new products and services. A linear process is not appropriate for today's highly competitive world, so most companies carry out the tasks associated with NPD simultaneously. For example, packaging design and initial planning for the international launch can be undertaken at the same time as consultation with selected worldwide partners and customers on the refinements needed to the product. Equally important is achieving faster market diffusion. This is achieved by using different market entry methods such as joint ventures and strategic alliances and improved marketing management techniques.

Perhaps the biggest challenge for companies is posed because it is becoming increasingly difficult and costly to achieve the 'next big breakthrough'. As a result companies are focusing on innovating throughout the company (processes, operations) in order to make improvements in everything they do. The most innovative and successful companies are able to encourage innovation and share good practice throughout the organisation.

Activity 10.4

Identify a new product that has been launched recently by your organisation or one you know well. Interview the manager responsible to determine:

- What lessons (good and bad) were learned about the NPD process, focusing particularly on the international dimensions?

- The extent to which the views of the staff and customers in international markets were included in the development and launch plans.

- What should be changed for the next new product?

Case Study – Levi Strauss

By the mid 1990s, with a turnover of $6 billion, there was no doubt that the USA West Coast based organisation, Levi Strauss, was a world leader in manufacturing and marketing jeans.

The product originally started life as a unique, riveted waste overall. In fact, the idea of rivets on the pockets was patented, and it was the only blue denim with this feature up until the early 1990s. In the 1930s the product had become the standard wear of the American cowboy, but it was not until the late 1950s that jeans developed as a cult phenomenon – worn by such matinee idols as Marlon Brando and James Dean. However, in the early 1980s a new clothes line became fashionable – that of the polyester suit – which contributed to a sales decline in denim.

All this changed with the arrival of Robert Haas, the Chairman and CEO. He took over when the company was at a low point in 1984. He gathered a lot of talented people around him and decided to refocus the company on its core product – the Levi 501 brand. He took a big gamble on a single product strategy that worked – due in some considerable way to the clever positioning strategy of its advertising. The advertising portrayed the gritty and urban image of 501s, with the backing of some appropriate blues music. In fact, the astute use of music has played a big part in the 501 strategy. The advertising showed real people doing real things and sales began to increase.

With the success, Robert Haas decided on a leveraged buyout of the company and decided to target international markets. The brief in London fell to the advertising agency BBH. The product was to move from a 'mainstream' to a premium product, with a focus on the Levi 501 brand as the original American blue jean. A string of successful advertisements (mainly based on sex appeal) including the famous Nick Kamen 'man in the launderette' advertisement, accompanied by great music, made the brand a runaway success. Levi's sales rocketed 800%, but strangely, so did those of other brand manufacturers, who did not spend a penny on advertising.

As a result of the successful advertising campaign, Levi's attained a premium position and was successfully able to charge a retail premium. The 501 brand sold for US $85 equivalent in London, $50 in New York and $30 in a discount store in San Francisco. Levi's were making a healthy profit on a product which was basically no different, nor expensive to make, than its competitor products. Like Pepé or Wrangler, the product was based on good quality control and good yarn.

In fact, in a 1993 consumer test report, the Levi's 501 was outperformed in many test categories by its competitors.

The challenge in the early 1990s was to maintain the number one global position in the world. How could a leading market producer stay in the dominant position? Rivals like Diesel had shown what could be done by being a niche player – being very successful in a narrow market niche. Levi's branched out into the 'Dockers' brand, which was a diversification built on the trend to smart office wear clothes. This was a good move to avoid the 'saturation' point which might be rapidly approaching for the mainstream brand. Levi's pioneered the concept of 'casual Friday', a new idea which allowed workers to attend their place of work casually dressed for one day each week. If it failed, Dockers would not harm the 501 main line, as it was promoted differently. Levi's also created their own stores to sell exclusively Levi's lines.

Robert Haas believed in a company culture not based on private jets and limousines, but on a code of ethics which made employees see themselves as stakeholders in the business – even if not actually a stockholder. However, this philosophy was put to the test with the closure in 1990 of one of the San Antonio sewing factories, and very importantly, the realities of the global were bought home – such as a need to stay cost competitive.

In early 1996, with a $1 billion cash surplus, Haas bought back even more stock and shares changed hands at 53 times their 1986 values. The company had reached a high point.

What a difference two years can make! In late 1998 it was reported that four European factories and two US plants were to close. A total of 1,500 staff in Belgium and France and 991 staff in the US were made redundant. Revenue had fallen to $3 billion and it just wasn't cool any more to wear Levi's jeans. Competition had taken its toll, with fashion item multinationals such as Calvin Klein and Lee Jeans brands doing well. Up-market jeans like Armani and Yves St Laurent were becoming the coolest jeans.

The company strategy in developing the Dockers brand and new rigid hard wearing denim, plus their emphasis on product focused advertising, suddenly seemed to be out of touch with current consumer tastes. For an historically successful international company faced with such a reversal of fortune, the major concern now is how to re-establish itself to its former leading position.

Source: *International Marketing Strategy* examination paper, December 1999.

Questions

1.   What environmental factors contributed to the 1998 position of Levi's?

2.   As a marketing consultant, what would you advise them to do in the three years following the article (1999-2002)? Give reasons for your answer.

SUMMARY OF KEY POINTS

- In terms of selecting a strategy for product entry and management, organisations can offer an existing product, supply what consumers are buying or design a product that will appeal to a global customer segment.

- Competitor activity may act as a constraint if the rival product is a strong brand in that country.

- Identity, branding and positioning in international markets are dependent on consumers' experience, preconceived ideas and expectations of the product and its COO.

- In NPD the key issues for international marketers to consider are the increasing speed of development, shorter life cycles and whether or not to centralise R&D.

Improving and developing own learning

The following projects are designed to help you develop your knowledge and skills further by carrying out some research yourself. Feedback is not provided for this type of learning because there are no 'answers' to be found, but you may wish to discuss your findings with colleagues and fellow students.

Project A

Design a product portfolio, from your own organisation's products, for an international market of your choice.

What modifications might you make to existing products to improve sales?

Do you have a global brand in your portfolio?

Project B

For the market identified above, what other new products might you wish to develop?

Project C

In many ways, football lends itself to globalisation as it is universally understood and to a large extent transcends cultures. The UK club Manchester United is recognised globally.

What advice would you give to one of your country's top football clubs if they were considering becoming a global brand?

Feedback to activities

Activity 10.1

- You should consider the environmental, customer and competition trends but focus particularly on the changes in the marketing response that is needed.

- In carrying out this activity you should also consider the trends in other industries that might, in time, affect your industry. What marketing lessons can you learn from this study?

- Against this background, what changes in product management should your company adopt?

Activity 10.2

It is important to remember that these are conceptual models that provide possible marketing strategies – they are not forecasting tools. Consequently, detailed evaluation of factors such as environmental factors, competitor activity, research and development capability, available resources and international marketing competence needs to be undertaken before decisions are made.

Activity 10.3

Companies must either build upon a positive COO effect or counter a negative COO as a basis to build their own brand and company image. Of course, this changes over time. Over the long term the perception of Japanese products, for example, has changed substantially. Short-term perceptions change for political reasons – such as anti-American or pro-American feeling in some countries, depending on actions undertaken by government.

Customers are also becoming more sophisticated about COO. They understand that the brand, the design, the component manufacture and assembly of a product may have different COOs.

Activity 10.4

From this you will discover the overall approach to R&D (centralised or decentralised). You should discover not only what lessons could be learned but also how the company will take the benefit from those lessons and how they might be learned throughout the organisation.

You might also ask about the length of time that it took to launch the product onto the markets around the world and the degree to which the NPD was undertaken within the company or in co-operation with outside organisations.

Session 11

Pricing decisions

Introduction

As an integrative part of the marketing mix, price plays an important role in influencing buyer behaviour and purchase decisions. Therefore, the different factors that need to be considered when developing pricing strategies are discussed in this Session.

LEARNING OUTCOMES

At the end of this Session you will be able to:

■ Discuss the factors affecting pricing decisions.

■ Develop a pricing strategy for international markets.

■ Explain the meaning and specifics of Incoterms.

■ Discuss currency considerations in exporting and international marketing.

Pricing often appears to be the most responsive, flexible, independent and controllable element of the marketing mix, but many managers consider that pricing decisions are complex and difficult to make.

Most companies recognise the importance of pricing at a tactical level, for example, for stimulating short-term demand, accelerating market entry or responding to competitive actions. However, far fewer companies value the strategic role of pricing in international marketing.

Pricing decisions are affected by internal factors such as the corporate objectives and the strategy adopted by the company, and external factors such as customer expectations, competitor strategies and the environment situation. For example, the market entry strategies that are based on low involvement in the country usually lead to a pricing strategy based on simply adding a profit margin to the costs incurred.

Higher involvement market entry strategies mean that the company will have much greater awareness of the market factors, such as the price customers are willing to pay, the prices charged by competitors and changes in, for example, the economic climate. This enables them to take a more strategic view of pricing.

Internal factors

The most obvious factor that affects pricing decisions is the costs incurred in the supply chain, including developing, producing and delivering the product or service to the customer, and providing support services in the market. We deal with the specific issues relating to costs in later sections of this Session but the most significant issue is in which countries the major components of costs are incurred, and what action can be taken to reduce them.

Expanding the scale of a company's operations through international marketing can enable it to take advantage of economies of scale and benefits resulting from the experience effect. It is also possible to reduce costs by relocating production and support services in countries with lower labour costs. As education and skill levels improve, ever more sophisticated operations tasks are being undertaken in emerging countries.

An example of company objectives affecting pricing strategies is the difference between Japanese companies taking a long-term view of profit generation from new market entry and companies from western countries that are typically under greater short-term pressure to generate profits and price.

External factors

External factors include the environmental factors, such as the stage of the economic cycle, the stage of the country's development and the laws affecting competition. Currency exchange rates and the problem of financing international deals in less developed countries are issues that will be dealt with later in this Session.

Competition varies in nature (for example local, international, own label), location (everywhere or in selected geographical markets) and intensity. Questions to consider include:

- Is the competition cut throat?

- How should the competition be tackled – head on?

- Is there an unofficial agreement between the largest players or even a cartel – which of course is illegal in most countries?

Customer expectations also vary and there may be certain countries where there is a greater willingness and ability to pay than others. A good example of these factors coming together was the decision of the South African government to insist that they pay pharmaceutical companies far lower prices for anti-Aids drugs than more affluent countries.

The most successful companies understand the implications of these factors but develop their marketing mix strategy based on an integrated approach between price and the other elements of the marketing mix. It is essential that organisations avoid falling into the trap of believing pricing to be an independent controllable variable within the marketing mix. Environmental and market factors play a significant part in developing a sustainable pricing strategy. As previously discussed, markets are becoming increasingly interdependent and so it is important to consider how a pricing strategy in one market might affect the pricing strategies in other markets, where the same competitors are present and customers have similar needs.

Activity 11.1

Prepare a PowerPoint presentation entitled 'Factors affecting international pricing decisions in our industry'.

Strategic approach to pricing

There are three approaches to international pricing strategies:

- Standardised or ethnocentric – setting a price at the factory gate and charging additional delivery costs to the customer.

- Adaptation or polycentric – locally set pricing.

- Geocentric pricing – a pragmatic combination of the two approaches.

The development of a pricing strategy involves the same steps of analysis, objectives setting, strategy development, implementation and then integration across markets as we discussed in the planning section. The pricing strategy objectives should be set against considerations about levels of demand in different markets and the company's response; for example, market skimming or penetration to increase market share, or pricing to prevent competitors entering the market. Clearly, without integration across markets the company may allow a competitor to build a company foothold in a number of local markets that could ultimately act as a springboard for the global market.

Influences on cross-country integration of pricing strategies

The importance of the effective cross-country integration of pricing strategies cannot be over-emphasised. Due to greater global activity competitors are more aware of differences in pricing levels. For example, multinational operators buying from a multinational supplier can easily compare the prices they are being charged in different markets by using the company's Intranet.

With increased travel and the increasing availability of information, particularly on the Internet, customers are more aware of differences in prices. Perhaps the most significant change for customers in Europe is the introduction of the Euro, the European single currency, which has had the effect of making cross-country pricing even more transparent and cross-border shopping more prevalent.

The result of increasing competition and better consumer knowledge is that prices are being forced down. Previous sources of differentiation of products, such as a global brand, high levels of quality and service are now taken for granted and no longer command the premium price they did. In response to this, managers must find new ways of adding value and exploiting new market opportunities. Many new opportunities appear to exist in LDCs but often, additional problems such as higher levels of risk set new management challenges which must be taken into account when developing international marketing strategies such as pricing.

Activity 11.2

Choose two or three products or services that you would consider buying personally, for example a DVD player, an airline ticket or a car.

Check the price using different web sites in different countries.

What pattern emerges from the prices that are offered, and what does this tell you about the pricing strategies adopted?

Exporting

In this section we look at building up the cost of goods that are being exported in order to consider what is the impact of transfer across country borders. Transfer across borders clearly incurs additional costs such as transport and tariffs, where appropriate. Without compensating factors this can mean that the exported product cannot compete on price when compared to local suppliers. Clearly, if the imported product is better quality, higher specification or can carry a brand premium, customers may still be prepared to pay the higher price. But what if the imported product is exactly comparable?

Firstly, the exporter might be able to reduce the cost (and thus the price) without reducing overall profit, because of the effect of additional export sales on contribution – particularly if the home market has reached saturation point. Secondly, the importer may charge for the product in local currency. A favourable exchange rate might initially help the importer to set a lower price in local currency without reducing profits.

Of course, currency exchange rates fluctuate and an unfavourable rate later would mean that keeping the same local price would lead the company to making losses. So what should the company do? Assuming that the company is charging the most it can for the product in the local market it only really has three options – none of which are really satisfactory:

- Maintain the price and lose money until the exchange rate becomes more favourable, but retain customer and distributor loyalty.

- Withdraw from the market until it is viable for the company to re-enter and risk losing customer loyalty.

- Raise prices significantly, lose sales volume and risk being seen to be exploiting customers.

Setting the final price in the market is critical because it should not just depend on the costs incurred but should also reflect the customer response to other marketing mix factors. A major pricing problem is faced by companies that wish to add value through providing customers with additional service, because it is difficult to predict the actual or perceived benefits to the customer of added service before starting. For example, a major oil company won a contract to provide a lubricants management system to a new car factory in Europe. Previously, when they had simply offloaded the lubricants at the factory they had charged in price per litre. With the new contract they simply raised the price per litre to cover the anticipated additional service. However, they (the oil company) proved to be very successful in managing the fluids and cut the amount required by 50%. In so doing, of course, they also reduced their anticipated revenue by 50%!

Incoterms and export quotations

In addition to the problems of fluctuating exchange rates there are other problems when transferring goods across borders. Transport, payment of tariffs and other taxes, and conforming to the country's legal and administrative requirements for imported goods all require managing and paying for. The exporter must negotiate with the customer to establish at what point the ownership of goods will be transferred and who will take responsibility for each stage.

The International Chamber of Commerce (ICC) has developed a number of Incoterms to help control the many uncertainties attached to the process of delivery:

- Ex-works (EXW) – in this case the contract specifies that the buyer takes ownership at the exporter's factory or warehouse so the exporter does not incur costs relating to delivery transport. The buyer therefore pays a lower price.

- Free on Board (FOB) – the exporter is responsible for the goods up to the point at which they are taken on board. The buyer has more control over the shipping line and insurance company used so can employ a domestic line, thus reducing the amount of foreign currency needed to finance the contract.

- Cost, Insurance, Freight (CIF) – the exporter is responsible for all costs and risks in delivering the goods to a destination port specified by the buyer.

A key question for many exporters is whether to price in local or domestic currency. Pricing in the domestic currency is advantageous for the exporter as the currency exchange risk is transferred to the customer, but, of course, the customer will typically want stability in the cost of its supplies and prefer to be charged in the local currency.

Finally, giving credit to customers in less economically stable markets is more risky and so exporters must take steps to protect themselves against the possibility of customers defaulting on payment.

Activity 11.3

Interview your transport manager and financial controller to find out about the alternative pricing approaches the organisation can use and the arguments for and against.

Problems associated with international pricing

What makes international pricing significantly different from domestic pricing is that it is necessary not only to set a price, recognising currency differences, but also to manage the financing of the deal. Issues of currency fluctuation, lack of hard currencies, transfer pricing and grey marketing all cause problems for organisations when they are implementing pricing strategies.

The problems associated with managing transactions across frontiers, for example, because of currency fluctuations and the increasing value of trade with countries lacking hard currency, means that the integration of financial management with international marketing are taking on a growing importance. There are a variety of strategies, which can be used to address these issues, but, as all of these responses to the problems have significant limitations, pricing problems can cause companies some of the greatest difficulties in international marketing.

Exchange rate problems

In the last section we introduced the problems of currency fluctuations for exporters. For multinationals currency fluctuations take on extra significance, because of the associated risk. They need to be managed in detail by forecasting likely trends – if necessary buying currency before it is required, in the expectation of adverse rate changes – and balancing the impact of fluctuations in the currencies in which supplies are paid for and goods charged.

Transfer pricing

A surprisingly large proportion of world trade is done within multinationals, through transfer between strategic business units. The price of the transfer needs to reflect the value of the goods, so that the governments of the countries involved can charge appropriate taxes. Companies attempt to manipulate the transfer prices so as to incur more of their tax bill in the country where taxation is lower and thus pay a lower overall charge. Whilst government taxation departments are becoming more effective in dealing with such manipulation by MNEs, services are much harder to tax, as due to their intangible nature, they 'cross' borders without easily being accounted for.

Grey marketing

Grey marketing is best explained as the distribution of products through distribution channels that are unauthorised by the company.

Goods may be more expensive in one country, perhaps because of taxation, lower demand and more tightly controlled distribution. In another country, a distributor of the product may have excess lower-priced stock available and might sell it through unofficial dealers to the customers in the country where higher prices prevail.

There are many examples of grey marketing around the world and it is not illegal. Volkswagen was fined by the EU for trying to prevent grey marketing within their dealerships by telling Italian dealers not to sell cars to people with addresses in Germany, where prices were higher.

Counter-trade

Trading with emerging countries presents MNEs with a final problem – that of not being paid in hard currency. At its simplest, the most ancient form of international trading – barter – is used, but this has significant disadvantages. Usually a more advanced form of counter-trade is used in international trade such as:

- **Compensation trading** – payment for goods is accepted as a combination of cash and goods.

- **Counter-purchase** – as it sounds, the seller agrees to sell goods locally at a certain price and in a simultaneous contract buys goods or services locally for an equivalent or proportionate payment.

- **Off-set** – similar to counter-purchase but national governments are involved.

- **Switch deals** – similar to barter but, in this case, the exchange goods are inappropriate. They are then exchanged in another country for ones that are acceptable.

- **Buyback** – for example, the cost of a capital purchase is paid for by goods produced from that capital equipment.

Interestingly, these counter-trade forms are being used increasingly in trade in developed countries for very high value contracts.

Activity 11.4

Re-read Doole & Lowe, 2001, *International Marketing Strategy*, 3rd Edition, pages 438-447.

Which of the pricing problems does your company suffer from? We have listed some problems in the table below to start you off.

What action is being taken to minimise their effect?

What more could be done?

Pricing problems	Nature of your company's problems	Action currently being taken	Possible further action
Setting a transfer price. Exchange rate fluctuation. Lack of hard currency in LDCs. Grey marketing.			

Case Study – A question of choice

At the end of November last year clothing giant Levi Strauss and supermarket giant Tesco found themselves confronting each other in court – and in the news. They both racked up column inches and made the national TV broadcasts with the kind of coverage that neither of them wanted or needed. Courtroom spats are never pretty.

On this occasion the winner was, for now, Levi's. The European Court of Justice ruled in its favour in its case brought against Tesco. For anyone who wasn't following it, Levi Strauss sought to prevent Tesco from importing Levi's jeans from outside the European Economic Union (EEU) to sell back into the UK at cheaper prices. In a judgement that will have implications for a wide range of goods from designer clothes to perfumes, the court ruled that Tesco was not allowed to sell Levi's jeans without the manufacturer's consent, which has so far not been given. Furthermore, Levi Strauss claimed that staff selling its products needed special training.

Mike Gilbert of patent and trademark attorneys Marks and Clerk explains the legal background to the case and future consequences. "Previously the law regarding parallel importation of goods into the UK from outside the EEU had been unclear.

A previous judgement in the English courts had meant that trademark owners, who had not placed express restrictions on the importation of their goods which were enforceable down the supply chain, were assumed to have consented to importation."

Not so any more. "This case means that goods may only be imported from outside Europe if the importer can show that the trademark owner has given up the right to oppose importation," says Gilbert.

According to media lawyer Colin Winter of Ingram Winter Green, this is far from the only case of its kind. "It's just one example of this type of case that flies around all the time, but it has caught people's interest because it is two well-known giants."

Winter reckons that, globally, parallel trading is now an enormous issue. He says, "Some people would see the parallel market as a form of price competition but there are good reasons why Levi's should be able to protect itself and its business."

Before the judgement, Tesco had been making many jeans wearers very happy by selling the Levi's brand at very low prices. For a time, it looked like the consumer was onto a winner and, indeed, before the court's verdict, Tesco was confident that it would win.

The judgement, when it came, had serious implications for not just Tesco but for the whole parallel trade industry as well as brand owners.

On one side of the debate there are the brand owners defending their rights over how they distributed their products; on the other, the parallel traders and the Consumer's Association (CA) are fighting for cheaper priced goods, amongst other things.

Both sides have big names behind them. The British Brands Group, whose director is John Noble, has 25 members ranging from food and soft drinks manufacturers to household goods and sportswear companies. Meanwhile Gary Lux, lawyer and spokesman for the Parallel Traders' Association, is not short on retail muscle either. He represents some 25 members including major retailers such as Kingfishers and – oh yes – Tesco.

Lux explains the Parallel Traders Association's viewpoint. "This situation is potentially damaging for Parallel Traders and the consumer because people are being deprived of the choice of where they buy their branded goods and at what price. The UK consumer has to pay more than their counterparts in the US or Asia Pacific.

When asked about the issue of branded goods needing extra sales support, Lux is swift and dismissive with his reply. "That argument just doesn't stack up for me. It amounts to price fixing." He maintains that it is "nonsense" to stipulate where a given brand should be bought. "What after-sales service is there in a bottle of perfume?"

Meanwhile the CA carried out a survey to determine comparative prices of goods in different countries. The results showed that in eight out of nine cases, European consumers paid more for branded goods than consumers in the US. The reason for this, claims the CA, is down to brand owners controlling which retailers sell their goods – and the ban on parallel trade.

The solution, says the CA, is for the European Commission to amend the existing trademarks directive to allow parallel trade to operate freely within Europe and provide consumers with cheaper branded goods. According to the CA, parallel trade already exposes how brand owner distribution agreements maintain higher prices for European consumers. If parallel trade was allowed to expand, so the argument goes, consumers would have greater choice about what price they pay for branded goods.

Needless to say, John Noble, director of the British Brands group, has a different opinion. He applauds the recent ruling and sees it as a well deserved vote of confidence in the integrity of the brand manufacturers. "It makes sense that the brand manufacturers who have invested so much in their brands should be able to sell their goods to whom they want and how."

Noble believes that brands contribute to overall economic growth and have an important role to play in driving innovation and competition. "There is a lot of investment in producing a better product and it takes skill and risk in order to build up that reputation. The brand owner should be able to dictate where products are sold."

Noble maintains that brands give the consumer more choice, not less. "At the moment the consumer can choose from the Levi's brand, buy DKNY jeans in London's West End, or buy cheaper jeans from a supermarket or a builder's merchant. Brands give us choice and if they didn't exist then the consumer would be left with nothing but cheap goods to choose from."

Noble also feels that if brands come into the store through parallel traders then there will be a drop in quality for the consumer because they are not interested in quality, only the deal.

Noble argues that the behaviour of the parallel traders is hypocritical. "They are not considering the wider implications. If the brand manufacturer loses money, this will have implications for innovation and make it more difficult for the UK to maintain manufacturing jobs. We need to have a wider take on this than simply lower prices."

Nick Cooper, managing director of BRG Market and Brand Strategies, a marketing brand consultancy, believes that brands have become even more important in recent times. "Brands will remain important as they represent an easy way for the consumer to assume a known quality (in an uncertain world)."

Were Levi's right to limit supply?

"Unfortunately, yes," says Cooper. "I say that because I actually like Tesco as a company and as a brand." Cooper says that if brand owners deliberately restrict distribution, they are taking a gamble that by sticking to that tight audience at their given price they will still get that sale. "It's arrogant but that is what exclusive brands should be about," he says.

Consumers still have the choice whether or not to buy at that price. It is not illegal or immoral for each manufacturer to decide the price. There will always be room for the cheaper brand."

Source: *Marketing Business*, March 2002.

Questions

1. As a marketing consultant, what pricing strategy would you advise Levi's to adopt in the UK following the judgement?

2. As consumers become more mobile, globally, how do you think brands need to adapt their pricing strategies? Give reasons for your answer.

SUMMARY OF KEY POINTS

■ Pricing decisions are influenced by both internal and external factors.

■ A pricing strategy for international markets must take into account what is happening in the international country in addition to the domestic environment.

■ Incoterms were developed by the ICC to help reduce the uncertainties surrounding delivery and identify the point at which ownership of goods transfers from exporter to buyer.

■ Currency considerations in exporting and international marketing include currency fluctuations and the means of financing transactions such as exporting and delivery.

■ When trading with emerging countries it may not be possible for them to pay in hard currency so contracts involving counter-trade are employed.

Improving and developing own learning

The following projects are designed to help you develop your knowledge and skills further by carrying out some research yourself. Feedback is not provided for this type of learning because there are no 'answers' to be found, but you may wish to discuss your findings with colleagues and fellow students.

Project A

Review the prices of new products recently introduced into your country by a foreign manufacturer that you are aware of.

What pricing strategy was adopted? How successful was it?

What criteria do you think was particularly important when the pricing decision was made?

(For example, when Microsoft introduced Xbox into Europe, New Zealand and Australia they priced it at a premium – following its highly successful launch in the US – to try to recoup money spent in bringing the product to market. Critics said that this was too high and they were proved right. The price was significantly reduced within a few weeks to stimulate sales.)

Project B

Use the Internet to carry out some research into companies that are doing business with emerging countries.

What problems are they experiencing and how are these being overcome?

Project C

If you had developed a new games console to rival the Microsoft Xbox, following a successful launch in your own country, which countries would you export to:

1. Immediately?

2. In the future?

What are the reasons for your choice?

Feedback to activities

Activity 11.1

A list of factors is not really sufficient to address this issue. You should consider and comment upon the relative importance of the factors. This will vary from industry to industry. In some sectors government controls are very important; in others strong competitive pressure or dominant customers may provide the greatest pressure.

Activity 11.2

The real question here is who is controlling the prices that the customer would pay. How much influence do the manufacturer and distributor have on the final price? The price can substantially affect the perception of the product in the customer's mind and, of course, customers can much more easily compare prices nowadays.

Activity 11.3

Clearly, the company's attitude to risk is important here, but marketing issues such as building a relationship with customers or distributors and making a competitive, profitable offer also need to be taken into account.

Activity 11.4

Some pricing issues, such as dealing with weak or fluctuating currencies, become a way of life for some companies that are used to working in emerging markets. For other companies that are not used to such markets these problems can be very significant. Often they lead to fundamental debates about whether the company can cope with short- or long-term uncertainty caused by these problems and whether the outcome is worth the risk.

Session 12

Managing communications

Introduction

This Session provides an overview of the issues facing organisations communicating across cultural borders.

Once again, the issues of standardisation versus adaptation are significant as cross-cultural differences are encountered.

LEARNING OUTCOMES

At the end of this Session you will be able to:

- Determine international marketing communications issues relating to international positioning strategies.

- Explain the different tools available for international marketing communications.

- Explain the importance of cultural differences and similarities for international marketing communications.

The role of international communications

At the outset it is worth highlighting the role of international communications, before going on to identify the challenges that are posed. It is useful to think of international communications as a two-way process – listening as well as telling or promoting and to think of it in terms of the following table, which identifies the different activity and the challenges that are posed in international marketing communications.

	Role	Challenge
External marketing.	Communicating with all stakeholders external to the company.	Managing an effective and distinctive positioning – despite different perceptions of stakeholders around the world.

	Role	Challenge
Internal marketing.	Communicating the company's strategy to its own staff.	Ensuring that staff in distant locations are clear about what is expected of them and maintaining loyalty to the company.
Interactive marketing.	Ensuring staff all around the world communicate effectively and appropriately with external stakeholders.	Ensuring effective communication and service standards are maintained across cultures.

Figure 12.1: Challenges facing global marketing communications

Given the remoteness of some SBU locations it is not unreasonable to expect that the staff of these locations will feel very distant from the headquarters and feel closer to suppliers, major customers and even competitors than their own organisation. The communication language, the business and social culture and even the industry jargon may vary just as much within the company as it does between the countries.

Communication with international external stakeholders

Clearly the major focus of international marketing communications is on its external stakeholders and here again it is worth thinking about three dimensions:

Communication	Role	Challenge
Corporate identity.	Convey to existing and potential stakeholders the standards and values of the company.	Maintain consistency of identity around the world and provide the 'entry ticket' to new markets.

Communication	Role	Challenge
Product and service positioning.	The traditional elements of promotion, building the brand, and selling the products and services.	Maximise short- and long-term revenue generation across all markets.
Relationship building.	Use of systematic contacts to build and maintain relationships with key stakeholders.	Treat all the key stakeholders as of equal value, no matter their location in the world.

Figure 12.2: Focus of international communications

Clearly, the main focus of the company's activity may be maximising revenue, profit, and return on investment in the short term. However, a major objective also must be to use the communication tools to reinforce the company's positioning, increase the brand value, and build a loyal following of customers. This is achieved by the effective use of communication tools as well as other elements of the marketing mix. The real challenge is to manage customer relationships at all levels – hence the emergence of Customer Relationship Management (CRM) software.

Although the company's international positioning is influenced by its use of the communication tools, it is ultimately determined by customer perceptions. Customer perception can be influenced negatively by failures of the company's communications (lack of co-ordination, inconsistent and unclear messages etc.) and by external factors, such as counterfeiting, parallel importing, adverse criticism from pressure groups and inappropriate associations, for example with politicians and governments of questionable morality.

Activity 12.1

Find out how consistently your corporate identity is communicated throughout the organisation. Obtain copies of literature, visiting cards, letterheads etc. from your subsidiaries around the world.

> Place all the items in front of you, then, taking the role of a customer, decide if this looks as though it comes from one company:
>
> - Does it appear to be well organised and communicate congruently and clearly?
>
> - Are the verbal and non-verbal communications (colour, design, style, logos etc.) consistent?
>
> - Are there merely the necessary modifications for cultural sensitivity?

Communication tools

The starting point for thinking about the tools that can be used to develop the international communications strategy is the market entry decision, as this will determine the degree to which a push strategy (promotion through intermediaries) or a pull strategy (typically mass advertising to consumers) is used. Quite often, companies that have successfully used a combined push and pull strategy in their domestic and adjacent markets resort to a largely push strategy in more remote locations.

The basic models of communications still apply here in the planning stage: for example, AIDA (Awareness, Interest, Desire, Action) and the 4Ms (Message, Media, Money, Measurement) but there are problems, particularly when trying to use a standardised approach (for example, pan-regional advertising).

One of the most effective product launches was Häagen-Dazs premium ice cream, which initially established a strategy of market entry using its own special outlets in the most fashionable places in Europe before using intensive distribution through supermarkets. This approach, supported by distinctive PR and creative and rather sexy advertising, created a high profile product with a brand premium. Of course, not everyone is prepared to pay a premium price for ice cream, especially as the concept and brand image will be perceived differently in different markets.

Using the tools

Managers can use the generic elements of promotion, such as advertising, public relations, sales promotion, sponsorship, direct marketing and a sales force to develop communications that inform and persuade. This must be done creatively to make the company's messages stand out from the competition and from all the surrounding 'noise' of the media in the different business and social cultures. This is addressed in the next section. Equally importantly:

- The specific communication tools such as television, radio, newspapers and posters may not be available or valued in the same way in different markets in different countries.

- The communication tools may vary considerably in distribution (for example some countries have largely regional rather than national newspapers), cost/impact ratio (posters are the traditional official communication route for news in some countries), and the ease of measurement of impact may vary considerably, too.

- Laws may prevent certain types of advertising (for example tobacco and alcohol, or advertising to children) and limit or prevent sales promotions (amount of product given away free).

- Cultural differences may mean that some promotional games and free gifts are preferred over others.

- Cross-cultural value of sponsorships may differ.

- Direct marketing depends on the availability of accurate addresses or possession of telephones and complete lists, and e-commerce upon computer ownership. The appropriateness of some communication tools is put into perspective given the suggestion that half the world has never made a telephone call and there are twice as many Internet users in New York as in Africa.

- Trade fairs and trade missions have a much greater value in international markets.

Factors that are outside the company's control, such as legal constraints (for example, limits on advertising to children), media availability (for example, the number of televisions per person), and aesthetic cultural factors affect the degree to which promotion can be standardised.

The company can control its own actions (for example, the balance of local nationals to expatriates in the sales force, the use made of PR and the budgets allocated) to promote a consistent image and message in order to build customer value through brand familiarity. However, much of the promotional programme implementation is undertaken in conjunction with outside agencies, such as advertising or public relations agencies. For the larger companies, the major issue is whether it is more appropriate to use an international, home country or host country agency.

Activity 12.2

For your organisation, or one you know that employs an international sales force:

1. List the various expectations the organisation has of the sales force. (Think, for example, of product knowledge, empathy with customers and providing feedback on the product or service).

2. What are the arguments for and against using a largely home country based sales force, a largely expatriate sales force or host country nationals to ensure these expectations are met?

3. Which approach does the organisation adopt and why?

Responding to cultural similarities

In marketing communications and promotion it is necessary to assess the appropriateness of standardisation and adaptation, bearing in mind the need to communicate relevant and creative messages in a cost-effective way to a range of audiences in different markets. It can be argued that it is cheaper to develop standardised cross-border communication campaigns because of savings from economies of scale that can be made in the creative work and in production, and from experience curve effects – transferring knowledge of what works and what does not work. However, this must be balanced against the greater local responsiveness that can be gained by adapting the communication for each market, by using specially prepared messages.

One significant issue is the extent to which the message is either concerned with promoting products that are:

- Already used by customers (existing demand).

- Familiar to customers (latent demand) but not available at present.

- Unfamiliar to customers who might require educating to appreciate a new concept (incipient demand).

Each situation will require an alternative marketing mix approach. For example, there are worldwide segments of buyers for luxury goods, soft drinks and computers that respond to similar promotional appeals. Products and imagery that are seen by global audiences, through films, television, sponsorship of sporting and cultural events and through visiting foreign countries, can create a pent-up demand for brands and products in emerging markets. The launch of products that might be treated as ordinary in developed markets may create excitement in those newly emerging consumer markets.

Responding to local differences

The mass marketing media, such as TV advertising, must be responsive to the local culture if it is to have impact. Audiences can respond with anger if companies disregard or offend their most closely held beliefs or ignore local values. If advertising does not appear to appreciate the local culture or way of life it will have little impact. This might mean that a pan-regional promotions manager might have to approve a local advertising campaign that makes an appeal to customers that he or she simply does not understand or appreciate!

Cultural issues need to be taken into account in the selection and management of sales forces, not only because they determine the effectiveness of the sales force in the marketplace but also because they can affect communications within the company. The balance between the use of head office staff, expatriates and local sales staff is likely to affect the efficiency of contacts with head office and the transfer of company knowledge, and the effectiveness of the local country sales operation.

Public relations can play a significant role in embedding the multinational within the local culture and community by a variety of actions. PR must also be used effectively to manage local crises that could damage the reputation of the whole company.

Activity 12.3

Referring to the table below, how does the promotional mix of your organisation vary between five different country markets?

	Country 1	Country 2	Country 3	Country 4	Country 5
Advertising Target audience Message Media used					

	Country 1	Country 2	Country 3	Country 4	Country 5
Sales force Role Composition					
Public relations Role Methods used					
Promotional Budget Emphasis* Measurement					

*You may not be able to get different budget allocations by country and media, but you should compare the overall level (low/medium/high) between promotion methods by country.

Case Study – Looking on the bright side

Successful advertising in the West rarely makes the journey to the Asia Pacific region. Many missed opportunities have come down to cultural differences: how language is interpreted differently in Asia Pacific, as well as cultural expectations and nuances. In Eastern cultures, nuance and tone is everything.

Many people in the Asia Pacific region make great use of negative expression; a reflection, some have argued, of their deep-seated thought processes. However, such negative modes of Eastern thinking simple reflect responses to situations that have deep cultural underpinnings.

For example, in the West, if someone asks 'How are you?', the typical response may be 'good' or 'fine'. However, when Western people say 'not bad' they in fact mean 'good'. In other words 'not bad' and 'good' are not opposites. They mean one and the same thing.

Conversely, when Eastern people, especially those in the Indian subcontinent, say 'not bad' they do not necessarily mean 'good' in the Western sense.

For many on the Indian subcontinent, their so-called negativity is part of an approach or attitude that transcends both 'good' and 'bad'. Saying 'not bad' in Asia often means 'neither this or that' – a state of neutrality or non-attachment. Anyone familiar with Buddhist principles will have a clearer idea of what this means.

Asia's so-called negative language is deeply entrenched. The Indian people have a fondness for negative expressions. For example, terms such as non-violence, non-greed and non-hatred all have deep roots in personal conduct, and are therefore seen as holding more power over overt action, which is more common in the West.

Interestingly, Westerners can see examples of non-feeling in their own language. The word 'unwavering' is often used to describe a frame of mind, although there is far more power in 'not wavering'. Similar examples are 'unblemished', 'irreproachable', 'unrelenting' and 'unforgettable'. So perhaps Westerners have more in common with their Asian counterparts than they suspect.

A negative appeal in advertising will warn consumers about an annoying, repulsive or uncomfortable situation that might be experienced as a result of not buying or using the advertised product. The argument the advert would be communicating is that if the product is purchased, then the negative situation would disappear.

For example, an effective advertisement for insect repellent would focus on the consumer's discomfort and annoyance before the product is purchased.

FMCG products are typically advertised in terms of 'not wanting or lacking in goodness and nourishment' rather than 'full of goodness and nourishment'. Here again, the absence of the negative is considered to be more vivid and tangible than the presence of the positive in the mind of the Asian consumer.

A typical advertisement for TV sets may talk about a product being 'free of distortion' rather than having a 'clear picture'.

The care with which positive expression is employed in Eastern advertising, especially in the Indian subcontinent, also illustrates the power of negative expression in this part of the world.

For example, the distinction between 'praise' and 'flattery' in the English language is less marked than in the Sinhala and Tamil languages chiefly spoken in Sri Lanka. In English, 'flattery' is merely expressive praise and still serves a legitimate purpose of gratifying or inspiring one. In the Sinhala or Tamil languages flattery is clearly praise overdone, which transforms it into something deceitful, false and empty.

This means that the positive expression should be used sparingly and with extreme care when promoting products in this part of the world.

Other distinctions also exist. In Western thought, there is enormous emphasis put on logic and rationality: that truth is out there if only we can find the right logical sequence. The Eastern view holds that problems are resolved quite differently; that one must wait for the 'truth' to appear, that it is not found by active searching or by deep rational reasoning. The major difference is one of attitude: one active, and the other passive. Do not underestimate these differences – they run very deep.

Western marketers must be far more aware of the differences in Asia's collective psyche if they want their advertising strategies to be more effective. But it is not just Western advertisers who are guilty of using inappropriate language when targeting an Asian audience. Many Eastern advertisers have blindly and thoughtlessly adopted Western models and paradigms. What works in the West does not always work in the East and vice versa. Globalisation does not work everywhere.

Source: *Marketing Business*, November 2000.

Questions

1. What advice does the Case Study give to advertisers contemplating launching a campaign in the East?

2. Why do you think the differences discussed 'run so deep'?

3. How could you ensure that your advertising campaign is culturally acceptable for the market it is aimed at?

SUMMARY OF KEY POINTS

- For organisations operating in a number of countries, internal marketing communications must ensure that each employee in every location understands the overall business objectives and communications.

- Communicating to external stakeholders across borders means that the message needs to be altered to take account of cultural differences but it must still communicate a consistent corporate identity.

- The communication tools must be appropriate for the country and this will depend on cultural acceptance, level of development and current usage of different media such as the Internet.

- New technology will have an increasingly significant impact on how information is communicated and shared globally, and will also impact on the ability of organisations to innovate processes and present their products to the market.

Improving and developing own learning

The following projects are designed to help you develop your knowledge and skills further by carrying out some research yourself. Feedback is not provided for this type of learning because there are no 'answers' to be found, but you may wish to discuss your findings with colleagues and fellow students.

Project A

Read Usunier, *Marketing Across Cultures*, 3rd Edition, 2000, Chapter 14, Box 14.1: The influence of religion on advertising in Saudi Arabia.

Look at the advertising your company produces and identify how it might have to be changed if it was to be produced in Saudi Arabia.

You may also like to look at other examples of advertising and do the same for these examples.

Project B

Read Usunier, *Marketing Across Cultures*, 3rd Edition, 2000, Chapter 14, Box 14.3: The internationalisation of Reader's Digest.

Which other magazines or journals are you aware of that have successfully internationalised?

How did they achieve this?

Project C

Discuss the impact that new technology has had on internal and external communications within the last five years with colleagues in your department and other parts of the organisation – including those separated from you by distance and time.

Feedback to activities

Activity 12.1

Customers that buy your products in different countries will easily become confused if your material lacks consistency. If you were to go into a McDonald's, KFC or Burger King restaurant where the colours used in the logos were faded and the design was very different from what you were used to, would you be concerned that the quality and service might also be less good?

Activity 12.2

The balance between use of expatriate and home country sales staff should depend very much on the nature of the industry sector, the complexity of the products and the company's strategy. Long-term assignments are considered very expensive and are now usually used only for top-level staff. Shorter-term assignments can be of greater value and, as part of the role, often include training local staff. As with all elements of communications the company has to achieve balance, integration and focus on developing an improved local performance.

Activity 12.3

Where substantial differences emerge you should work out why this is. Is there strong market justification for the differences, or are there strong internal factors – an influential manager, for example!

Where there are differences, the market justification might be different – being based on customer response levels to different promotional tools. By contrast, you may be targeting a customer segment that responds similarly to the same communication tools and so your promotion activity might be the same and the budget allocated proportionate to the number of customers or sales.

Session 13

Relationship marketing

Introduction

The importance of building effective and long-term relationships with your customers has been a core feature of business-to-business marketing for some time. It is now recognised that it is also essential in all sectors because of the decline in customer loyalty and the cost of replacing lost customers. As you will appreciate after studying this Session, international marketing is no exception.

LEARNING OUTCOMES

At the end of this Session you will be able to:

■ Discuss relationship marketing as a strategy.

■ Discuss relationship marketing as an alternative to the traditional marketing mix approach.

■ Discuss operational and tactical issues of relationship marketing.

■ Explain the cultural and people aspects of relationship marketing.

■ Describe some of the global technological developments and their strategic competitive effect, for example e-commerce.

The concept of relationship marketing

Various writers have undertaken research into customer satisfaction and customer retention and the ideas that come from these are encapsulated in two simple observations:

■ If a customer is satisfied with a product or service they will tell four other people, whereas if they are dissatisfied they will tell twenty.

■ The cost of winning new customers is usually many more times more expensive than retaining the customers that you already have.

The problem is that satisfying customers and retaining them is considerably more difficult in international markets – for reasons we will look at later.

The marketing solution to this problem is relationship marketing. It has been defined in a number of similar ways, for example:

- The role of relationship marketing is to identify, establish, maintain and enhance relationships with customers and other stakeholders, at a profit, so that the objectives of all other parties involved are met; and that this is done by a mutual exchange and the fulfilment of promises.

(Grönroos, 1990)

- The remit of relationship marketing is to form and sustain mutually beneficial relationships by bringing together the necessary partners and resources to deliver the best possible perceived value proposition for the customer.

(Peck, 1996)

In order to achieve effective relationship marketing, it is necessary to bring together the three strategic principles shown in Figure 13.1.

The relationship marketing concept

Figure 13.1: The relationship marketing concept

In organisations devoted to relationship marketing, the prevailing culture is such that:

- The overall marketing strategy and management driving the company's customer, product and service development is focused on improving the customer relationship.

- The objective of relationship marketing is to satisfy customers, so that they have no reason to change suppliers; therefore, the whole emphasis is placed on providing additional services that are perceived as valuable by the customer.

- Underpinning the whole approach is a philosophy of thinking of interactions as processes that can be made more efficient and effective for both the company and the customer through continuous quality improvement.

Supporting relationship marketing is the idea that a closer partnership between members of a supply chain can improve performance for both parties as they seek to work together to solve problems.

So why has relationship marketing become more important?

A number of changes have taken place in the international environment, including:

- More competition in a saturated market, so differentiation of the standard product and service offering is becoming more difficult.

- More concentration of purchasers amongst retailers and distributors – so fewer, more valuable opportunities to sell.

- Greater performance pressures driving customer expectations ever higher.

- More knowledgeable and demanding customers.

- Less loyal customers, willing to switch to new suppliers.

- Changing patterns and roles in the purchasing process.

- The effect of IT on the purchasing process and the supply chain.

- Power shifts in the distribution chain closer to the consumer.

- Changing customer expectations, and more subjective measures of quality and service.

- The breakdown of barriers between purchasing segments.

The benefits of relationship marketing are clear in b2b marketing. Many products are highly specific to the customer so relationships between supplier and customers are much closer and developed over time. The concept has also been applied to consumer marketing too but, for low-price items, the question has to be asked: why would consumers want a relationship with an MNE and in whose interest is the 'relationship'?

Activity 13.1

Achieving an appropriate relationship for the level of interaction that you have or wish to develop with your customer is key. Use the diagram below to decide the stage you have reached in your relationship with the stakeholders of your business unit.

Is this level appropriate for the business you do together and wish to do in the future?

BARE BONES: the product or service that we offer is all you need; you're free to buy it.

↓

REACTIVE: call me if you need me or if you have any problems and I'll see what I do.

↓

ACCOUNTABLE: I'm calling to see if everything's okay.

↓

PROACTIVE: I can enhance your use of the product or service. Let's talk so that we understand each other more fully.

↓

PARTNERSHIP: I want to help you succeed in every way.

Relationship marketing in an international context

The traditional approach to international marketing is underpinned by the dimensions of traditional marketing, and is built upon a series of discrete transactions, supported by the marketing mix elements.

It is based on the idea that customers are free to choose from any supplier but will be influenced in their decision by the marketing mix: the total product and service offer, brand appeal, promotional message, the availabilty and the price for the product and service. By contrast, relationship marketing is based upon continual interactions and the building of a closer relationship between parties built on mutual understanding.

Companies have found that, in many situations the traditional marketing approach is now less appropriate to their needs. They have found that future success is based more upon building the relationships at all levels of the company with their suppliers, customers and other key stakeholders based on customer satisfaction. The development of relationship marketing is best illustrated in the car manufacturing sector, where co-operation between the car manufacturer and its component and service providers has led to increased outsourcing. This has, in turn, led to the enhancement of the service role of the component maker from fabricator of parts according to a drawing provided by the car manufacturer, to the component maker undertaking research, design and development of the part.

So building customer satisfaction is no longer achieved by negotiating a good 'deal' in the traditional way. Whereas the negotiation was carried out between the salesperson of the selling company and the purchasing office of the purchasing company, in relationship marketing all levels and functions of the two companies interact in order to achieve an effective business relationship. Thus, every interaction should contribute to delivery efficiency and effectiveness.

Evaluation of this is best achieved by using the concept of the value chain as a way of adding value in all of the company's operational activities, both internal and external, and this is dealt with in the next section.

Payne, Christopher, Clark and Peck (1995) have suggested that success in the external market results from identifying and building the company's most important relationships with their stakeholders in the external market. They also identify six markets – **internal, referral, influence, employee, supplier, customer** – and suggest that the company must determine how these markets contribute to achieve success.

Activity 13.2

Using the six market model represented in Doole & Lowe, *International Marketing Strategy*, 3rd Edition, Chapter 10, Figure10.11, page 366, compare the emphasis placed on relationship markets in your organisation.

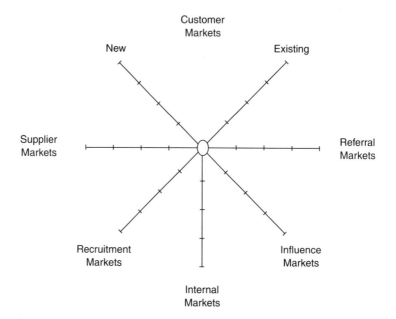

Plot on the diagram the importance that is currently given in your organisation to all six markets.

On which of these areas might the organisation usefully concentrate to develop its international business?

Relationship management chain

At the heart of relationship marketing is the relationship management chain, based upon the supply chain – the process by which the activities of internal departments and functions and the contributions of the external stakeholders are integrated to deliver an effective solution for the final customer. The concept of the relationship management chain is widely used to consider how value is built from a chain of internal and external contributions, and affected by the strategy, systems, culture and competences of those contributors. The contributions add value for the customer by: defining the value proposition, developing an appropriate segmentation, targeting and positioning strategy, achieving effective operations and distribution and establishing a measurement and control system.

Re-evaluating the way in which customer value is added through relationship marketing compared to traditional marketing means that emphasis should be placed differently. For example, in transaction marketing the competitive advantage for the company is based usually on the attributes of the product, whereas in relationship marketing the competitive advantage is based on relationship building and continuous improvement. A new or more differentiated product might be one outcome of improved relationship marketing.

Marketing mix in relationship marketing

The marketing mix must change. For example, mass advertising is undifferentiated and intended to persuade a proportion of the audience to respond, whereas relationship marketing requires targeted communications to be designed to persuade individual people or companies to respond in a particular way.

It is a redefinition of customer service and satisfaction. At this point it is necessary to highlight the difference between customer service and customer satisfaction. The first developments in improving customer service came in the US as companies realised that they were losing out to Asian companies in terms of quality. The US response was to improve customer service, develop company missions focused on service and quality and reinforce these activities through intensive staff training. Customer service, addressed in this way, is simply an add-on to the standard marketing mix elements of product, price, promotion and place. It can be argued, therefore, that customer service has the responsibility for putting right mismatches between the standard product offered and delivered, and the real customer needs and expectations.

Whilst customers are promised (and sometimes receive) high levels of service, there is no real guarantee that the products and services that they are offered deliver real customer satisfaction because they were not designed with the needs of any specific individual in mind.

Consequently, a model of marketing is needed that puts customer satisfaction first. A very flexible marketing mix must then be created so that the product offer can be modified to suit individual customer needs.

Activity 13.3

Select one product or service that you offer and prepare a simple flow chart of inputs – for example, research, product development, component manufacture, assembly, logistics etc. – right through to the consumer.

Think about the value that each process is adding and the cost to the customer. Think particularly about the contribution of distribution channel members. For the margin that they take, does the customer obtain reasonable value?

Does your organisation obtain benefits – such as promoting the product on your behalf, feeding back market information and so on?

Understanding customer satisfaction

So how can companies build a flexible marketing mix around providing customer satisfaction? The first challenge is to understand what equates to customer satisfaction in different markets around the world and the second challenge is to reorganise the service elements of the mix to deliver satisfaction and ensure that company-wide customer satisfaction is the main focus.

Consider the following questions that move the company beyond the traditional analysis tools of measuring customer service, into the area of really understanding what customers want and then benchmarking the service against the best providers.

- What measures of service and quality are really important to customers around the world?

- How does the company perform in this respect compared to its competition?

- Who are the leaders in providing customer satisfaction and how does the company perform against them?

- In which areas is the company strong and weak and how have the key measures changed with time?

Underpinning the action that is needed to address these questions is improved customer knowledge, and this can be achieved through better management of customer data and faster and more personal communications using appropriate communications media. Internet and Intranets integrated with effective databases make it easier to segment the market accurately, provide tailor-made products, target promotion, design finance/price packages and set up responsive distribution channels and logistics. As we have indicated, CAD, CAM and operational planning allow customised products and services to be offered. Electronic business allows very fast interactive communications that enable very high levels of service to be offered.

In the b2b sector and in manufacturing the supply chain is driven by web enabled communications to control purchasing, inventory management, delivery and so on. Having an effective electronic business strategy is essential for an international product or component supplier. Food retailer Safeway has a system that allows suppliers to check themselves if their products are out of stock in any store, so that they can arrange delivery and ensure good customer service. The b2c sector initially grew because of new electronic commerce businesses, such as Expedia and Lastminute in the travel industry, that did not rely on physical fulfilment of orders. However, traditional businesses, such as Tesco then started to operate both the physical and electronic retailing routes. Amazon, which marketed itself as the virtual bookstore and relied on suppliers to stock books for them, has now expanded its own facilities for stocking fast-selling books.

Customer service must now be available 24 hours a day, 7 days a week in many sectors. A GE medical machine was needed to scan an injured child late at night in California and the machine had a problem. The hospital rang the company's service centre in Milwaukee, which routed the call to Paris where a software engineer was available and fixed the problem in 30 minutes.

Delivering customer satisfaction

Relationship marketing is concerned with adding value for customers, particularly in markets that are highly competitive and essentially commoditised. New technology can assist in global 1:1 marketing described by enabling databases to be built which allow very specific targeting supported by very personal communications and promotion. One of the best-known examples is Amazon.com, the Internet book retailer.

Very precise targeting is possible through data mining – searching for customers or groups with very specific characteristics. The target consumers can then be identified, and then offered specific products that they are likely to buy.

Because the Internet allows all businesses to very easily gain access to their potential customers, it is possible for small companies to appear over the Internet to be 'on equal terms' with their large competitors and thus rapidly build their business by having closer and more effective relationships with customers. This is effectively what Amazon.com did.

For some companies relationship marketing will be of minor importance. Customer loyalty will be built through traditional methods and the cost of using very high levels of customer contact may not generate sufficient additional revenue. Their customers may not want a relationship with the company. Equally the staff may work more effectively in the 'cut and thrust' of transactional marketing. For other companies, particularly those involved in business-to-business marketing, relationships will be critically important for the future. The framework underpinning relationship marketing also provides the guidelines for businesses using e-commerce as a major tool in their marketing strategy.

Communicating effectively

New technologies enable marketers who are separated by distance, time and organisation to communicate at any time. Examples include:

- Mobile telephone.
- Email.
- Teleconference.
- Video conference.
- ISDN links.

What new technologies are used effectively in your organisation?

Activity 13.4

To achieve high levels of customer satisfaction and so build up long-term relationships, you really need to understand in detail how customers use your product, what they think about your product and how their purchasing processes work. You need a good understanding of the social and business culture in order to develop a meaningful relationship.

Interview a manager who deals with international customers. Prepare a list of the elements of a good relationship. Find out the importance that the manager places on the different elements of the relationship.

The impact of new technologies

As with many new technologies that are introduced, there is a temptation to conclude from the promotion associated with the technology that our lives and buying patterns will be changed completely overnight! In practice, change in customer buying patterns rarely takes place quite so quickly as might be expected, usually because the diffusion of technology into everyday activities and applications is often slow. Many dotcoms found out the hard way that e-commerce was not going to replace high street shopping totally or quickly.

The Internet has already changed the way that businesses and other organisations interact, communicate and do business with each other. In the business-to-business (b2b) sector there is a continuing revolution as the Internet offers the possibility for making efficiencies in business operations and communicating more effectively with other supply chain members. The real benefits are extremely fast transfer and sharing of information, so dramatically improving, for example:

- Placing and fulfilment of orders.

- Faster and more effective supply chain co-operation.

- The contribution to design and development of new products and services by a wider range of stakeholders.

- Progress chasing of production and delivery.

- Faster analysis and response to customer purchasing trends.

The benefits of the new Internet-based business-to-consumer market (b2c) was oversold to consumers in the late 1990s, causing hysteria in the stock markets of the world and huge over-valuations of dotcom businesses. In practice, many consumers with computers and Internet connections have now started to benefit from online retailing and other services but many others are still cautious. Companies have been able to use low-cost market entry strategies for untried markets in addition to their traditional channels. Others have been able to cut out the distributors and retailers that offered little contribution to the supply chain and customer perceived value. So what are the keys to success with Internet-based communication and commerce, and what are the problems?

The success factors for e-commerce include:

- A logical, informative, interesting, interactive and responsive web site.

- Integration of e-commerce with the traditional elements of marketing, especially physical distribution for products.

- Maintaining a 24 hours per day, 7 days per week service.

- Being customer responsive but not intrusive.

Some of the problems associated with e-commerce are:

- Over-optimism in the rate of conversion of new users.

- Data security problems, especially with credit card payments.

- Data protection and the ease of passing on information.

- The susceptibility of computers to system failure and corruption, hackers and viruses.

Despite the problems, Intranets and the Internet will have the most important effect on international marketing. The key challenge for businesses is to develop an integrated business model between the traditional and e-commerce routes to the market that is appropriate for the company, and the market in which it is operating, and is based on the key challenges facing international marketers.

In addition, the model must include adding customer perceived value and removing unnecessary costs to ensure competitiveness.

Case Study – Marketing through reconciliation

Fundamental mistakes are still being made even at the most basic level of cross-cultural communication. In many cases this originates from simple language differences. For example, when GM introduced the Chevy Nova, it was unaware that 'no va' means 'no go' in Spanish. As a result, sales in Spanish-speaking countries were extremely poor. Another simple but common example of cultural differences can be found in the different responses to different colours. The colour red often means danger in Western cultures, but can send different messages about the product to the Chinese, for whom red can also represent success. Similarly, yellow as a colour in marketing promotions may be offensive to Arabs, yet conveys freshness and summer to Western cultures.

More important than these overt and more obvious aspects of culture, are differences that derive more subtly from the different meaning given by different cultures to exactly the same thing.

For example, Americans may purchase a Sony Discman because it enables them to 'listen to their favourite music without being disturbed by others'. The Japanese may purchase the same product in order to 'listen to their favourite music without disturbing others'. The product may be identical but the purchasing motive is different, because of the different meanings and priorities given to one's own and others' privacy. The marketing message used to sell this product in each country would be notably different.

Kodak introduced an advertising campaign in the UK based on capturing 'memories' in the physical form of photographs. In contrast, for European cultures, 'memory' is a much more sentimental construct and may be tainted if represented in the explicit format of a photograph that omits the higher levels of experience.

Procter & Gamble had successfully developed a new generation of highly absorbent Pampers with the unique selling point that they could be changed less frequently. This approach failed in Japan where frequent changing is perceived as fundamental to keeping a baby clean.

A new methodology from Fron Trompenaars and Peter Woolliams addresses these challenges affecting global marketing. The approach is based on the three 'Rs': recognise, respect and reconciliation:

- **Recognise** – whilst we can more easily recognise explicit cultural differences, we may not be aware of these implicit cultural differences. This explains why this cultural diligence is usually absent from the management agenda and from the many classic marketing models such as Porter. Thus the first step is to recognise that there are cultural differences.

- **Respect** – different orientations about 'where I am coming from' are not 'right or wrong', they are just different. It is still all too easy to be judgmental about people and societies that give different meanings to their world from ours. Thus the next step is to respect these differences and accept customers' rights to interpret the world (and our products and marketing efforts) in the way they choose.

- **Reconciliation** – because of these different views of the world, we have two seemingly opposing views of the contrasting cultures – those of the buyer and seller. The task of the marketer is to reconcile these seemingly opposing differences.

We can categorise the different dilemmas that arise in each of several dimensions, based on our earlier research on cultural differences.

1. Do we follow a single global approach, or particularise to each market?

The dominant dilemma originating from this dimension is the global-local dichotomy. The question is, shall we have one standardised approach or shall we go for a local approach? Do we think our customers are best served by becoming nearly globally universal and alike, or becoming more influenced by particular national or local cultures?

The answer lies in transnational specialisation. Here we recognise the seemingly opposing extremes. We integrate best practice and satisfy customer needs by learning from the diversity of adopting, adapting and combining the best.

McDonald's successfully achieved this integration by branding the Big Mac universally across the globe. The big 'M' sign represents the universal corporate identity with standard furnishings and fittings in all their restaurants. Yet in the Middle East, the Big Mac is a veggie-burger, and is served with rice rather than fries in the Asiatic region. Even smaller local variations are promoted, such as the 'croquette' variant in the Netherlands.

Heineken alters the temperature at which its beer is served to follow local tastes but it also positions its same product differently in different markets – to reflect the different meaning that drinkers ascribe to the product. In Europe, it is sold as 'a beer that is meant to be drunk'. In the Caribbean, it is positioned as being 'cosmopolitan'. The (almost) identical TV advertisements for each island show the same shots of Paris, London and Tokyo (to represent the global branding of Heineken) but with an easily recognisable island-specific building or monument to locate the global brand in the local context.

In some situations, the marketing strength derives from the universal world branding. Thus Coca-Cola is Coca-Cola everywhere and represents the American dream, although details such as ingredients on the can or bottle may be in a local language. Similarly, British Airways is selling safe, reliable quintessential Britishness, supported by local agents in the different destinations it serves.

2. Individualism or 'communitarianism'

In the same way, this second dimension gives rise to a number of key dilemmas. Is marketing concerned with satisfying individual customer needs and preferences, or is the focus on creating a trend or fashion that is adopted by the group? Individuals then purchase to show that they have joined the group by following the shared trend.

From the customer's perspective, do we relate to others by discovering what each of us individually want, or do we place ahead of this some shared concept we can identify with or feel part of?

Simply rejecting the other viewpoint or adopting compromise will not yield the best market return. In our new marketing paradigm, we can follow the same logic for each dimension, by starting from one extreme, but integrating with the needs of the other.

Thus, although marketing to an individualistic culture might see the individual as an end, marketing will benefit from a collective arrangement as the means to achieve that end. Conversely, marketing to a communitarian culture sees the group as the target market, yet can use feedback and suggested improvements from individuals.

The marketing relationship should be seen as circular. The decision to focus on one end is only arbitrary.

Microsoft Windows and its associated Microsoft Office products offer the benefits of a group approach. Documents can be shared and exchanged, because they adhere to common file formats. Yet individuals can tailor the configuration of their system to satisfy individual preferences – such as the screen zoom level – to meet their individual eyesight capabilities. Jaguar and Mercedes owner-drivers take pride in being a member of their fellow club of drivers of prestige cars (belonging to their peer group). However, when they insert their individual key in the lock of their own car, the seat and the driving mirror configures to their own preference, even though someone else might have altered these settings.

At the meta-level we see how Richard Branson has successfully reconciled the personalities of 'David and Goliath' in the branding of Virgin. He successfully creates public sympathy in favour of the wronged individual confronting the collective assailant (the establishment).

3. Specific or diffuse

What is the degree of involvement of the customer? Do we see the customer as a 'punter', someone from whom we can make a fast buck, or is a customer a series of relationships over time? Do we need a relationship first, before he/she becomes a customer, or do we easily do business, from which a relationship may or may not follow?

With British Airways and American Airlines, we can examine how they each differently define their relationship with their customers. It is typically American to emphasise 'core competencies' and 'shareholder value'. In contrast, British Airways (and Cathay Pacific) emphasise service, with hot breakfasts and champagne. In a 'one world' alliance, it may appear that the options are limited to:

- Serve the 'cattle' with Coke and pretzels.

- Serve hot breakfasts and champagne and add in-flight massage and shoe-shine (and go bankrupt in the process).

- Compromise and sell the 'hot pretzel', thus upsetting (and losing) all customers.

Marketing through reconciliation is more than this. It is the craft of trying to define those specific areas to provide a more personal service and therefore deepen the relationship. Jan Carlson of SAS calls this the 'moment of truth'. The future success of an alliance will depend on one particular reconciliation: the competency of the marketing team to identify those specific circumstances where specific moments can be used to deepen the relationship in the service being provided.

4. Neutral or affective

What part does the display and role of emotion play, and/or is the display of emotion controlled?

Typically, reason and emotion are linked or combined. When the customer expresses satisfaction (or dissatisfaction), they are trying to find confirmation of their thoughts and feelings – and trying to show they have the same response as others ('I have the same view of this product/service as you'). Customers whose response is neutral, are seeking an indirect response.

Michael E. Porter claimed that Germans don't know what marketing is about. In his American conception, marketing is about showing (overtly) the qualities and features of your product without inhibition. Germans might see this as bragging, and the sort of tactic that might be expected from second-hand car dealers. The way you express positive things in Germany needs to be more subtle. As Tom Peters said in Atlanta in 1999, 'It's cool to be emotional nowadays'.

5. Achievement or ascription

Does the customer want a functional product that achieves the utilitarian purpose, or are they buying status? You can tell the time just as well from a $1 LED digital watch as with a $10,000 Rolex Oyster. But the latter is a symbolic representation of status, not simply a watch.

All societies give certain members higher status than others, signalling that unusual attention should be focused on those persons and the products they own and display and the services they consume.

In the achievement-oriented cultures, the emphasis is on performance. In ascribed cultures, such as Asia, status is ascribed to products that evoke admiration from others, such as high technology and jewellery. The status is more concerned with the functional capabilities of the product.

We can see the dilemma in action between the achieved and ascribed status in the profit-oriented versus non-profit oriented status of BUPA, reconciled successfully by CEO Val Gooding. Should she set a goal of 25% profit to shareholders to compete on the Stock Exchange, or make enough return to serve the sick and the weak? To care about people you serve is the precursor to success and you must ascribe the status to them.

The provident status of BUPA reconciles the need to achieve business growth with the need to provide primary healthcare. Care for your employees through a strong successful business and they pass that care to the clients (patients).

6. Internal and external control

Are we stimulated by an inner drive, or do we adapt to external events that are beyond our control?

The main issue here is to connect the internally controlled culture of technology push (sell what we can make) with the externally controlled world of market pull (what we can sell).

Nobody would deny the great knowledge and inventiveness of Philips in (separately) its technologies and the quality of its marketing. The problem is that these two major areas don't seem to connect. The push of the technology must help you decide what markets you want to be pulled by, and the pull of the market must help you know what technologies to push.

7. Time

Do we view time as sequential or synchronous?

With sequential cultures, time is an objective measure of passing increments. The faster you can act and get to the market, the more effective will be your competitiveness. In contrast, synchronous cultures like doing things 'just in time' so that present ideas converge on the future. The better your timing, the more competitive you will be.

Keeping traditional products that made your name in the first place can jeopardise the creation of new products. Karel Vuursteen of Heineken successfully integrated the (past) traditions of the Heineken family with the future needs of the company, and the traditions of the Heineken product with the need for (future) innovation – for example in the area of speciality beers. Process innovation sought new methods of creating the same result (a traditional product), while product innovation allowed new drinks to be produced from scratch without involving Heineken's premium products in the experiments.

Our new marketing paradigm requires a mindset that reconciles these continuing dilemmas. It is the result of linking learning efforts across each dimension with the contrasting viewpoint.

Source: *Marketing Business*, September 2001.

Questions

1. What advice is given to organisations on achieving customer focus?

2. What factors relating to consumer behaviour identified in the Case Study might you, as a marketer, need to consider if pursuing a policy of relationship marketing in a multinational enterprise?

SUMMARY OF KEY POINTS

- Relationship marketing is now an important competitive strategy for organisations as customer loyalty levels decline.

- The traditional marketing approach involving a salesperson and a purchasing manager is being replaced by interaction between all levels of the organisations on both sides – customer and supplier.

- Relationship marketing requires organisations to take a flexible approach to developing the marketing mix, so that specific customer requirements can be met.

- Operational processes and tactics must be focused on building a long-term relationship with the customer, which requires paying attention to detail in the short term.

- If relationship marketing is to be the main competitive thrust for the organisation, satisfying the customer must be a priority for everyone in the organisation – underpinning the prevailing culture.

- In the international markets, new channels of communication enable transactions to be completed smoothly and quickly.

- New technologies offer new opportunities for international marketers to reach customers – but just because it is there and new, it doesn't have to be used exclusively!

Improving and developing own learning

The following projects are designed to help you develop your knowledge and skills further by carrying out some research yourself. Feedback is not provided for this type of learning because there are no 'answers' to be found, but you may wish to discuss your findings with colleagues and fellow students.

Project A

Within your organisation how effectively are customer relationships managed:

i)   Internally?

ii) Externally?

iii) Across borders?

Project B

Review the customer loyalty programmes that have tempted you to remain constant to specific brands.

How effective have the organisations been in anticipating changing needs?

If it is a global brand, what aspects of the loyalty programme are 'local' to your country?

Project C

Choose the web sites of two companies; ideally competitors of your organisation, but otherwise customers or suppliers. Adopt the perspective of an international customer.

- List the criteria that you consider to be important in assessing the effectiveness of a web site.

- Rank each web site for each of the criteria on a scale of 1-5 (1 = good; 5 = poor).

- Assess your own organisation's web site from the perspective of an international customer.

- What pattern emerges from this? How should your own web site be improved?

Feedback to activities

Activity 13.1

Building relationships does not require time and resources to be invested in visible ways but, often, the cost is not fully appreciated. The cost of transactional marketing programmes – for example, an advertising campaign – is easier to calculate.

It is imperative that you do not invest too much time and resources in some stakeholders who you like but are not important, and too little on stakeholders who are important, but difficult to deal with.

Activity 13.2

Understanding these markets can be very important, particularly for MNEs. This is because their power in the foreign market is often achieved indirectly, for example through referral by experts or suppliers. The organisation may well underestimate the value in some countries, for example, of the reputation it builds for recruiting the best staff and the impact this has on existing and potential customers.

Activity 13.3

As changes take place in the environment and market, the value of the contributions might change. A number of companies (e.g. in the travel industry), have replaced intermediaries by e-commerce (so called disintermediation) as a way of becoming more cost-effective.

Activity 13.4

You should also find out the degree to which the relationship depends on a small number of executives within the business or whether relationships have been built throughout the organisation. This, of course, is important because in some cultures the individual contact is critical, and if a particular contact is broken the relationship may be lost.

Session 14

Place in international marketing

Introduction

Getting to the customer is fundamental in all types of marketing, so this Session explores this issue from the international angle.

LEARNING OUTCOMES

At the end of this Session you will be able to:

- Select appropriate international distribution and logistics strategies.

- Explain how to manage channel relationships and customer service expectations.

- Discuss trends and recent developments in distribution in international markets.

- Explain how to develop an international salesforce.

Issues relating to global distribution

In global marketing, the strategic and tactical use of distribution channels to gain competitive advantage is imperative because the channels of distribution provide the greatest source of customer contact, but this requires a high level of financial resources. Efficiency and cost effectiveness are therefore essential.

Moreover, members of the distribution channel usually require long-term commitments by the manufacturer or service provider to justify the investment of time and resources. The long-term nature of distribution decisions forces a careful analysis of future developments in the distribution channel. If new forms of distribution are emerging (for example, mass merchandise retailing or Internet retailing), this has to be considered early in the planning stage of the distribution channel. The consequences of wrong decisions made by companies when making such long-term commitments can be highly significant if the market is rapidly changing.

Frequently, the market entry strategy chosen will determine the distribution and logistical options available to companies. Because the distribution channels of countries have often been developed in response to their different traditions and cultures, companies rarely have a free choice in developing distribution strategies, but instead have to fit their strategy to the country's infrastructure.

Country differences

The distribution system of a country can vary enormously. In Finland, there are four centralised wholesalers covering the whole market for most product categories. In Japan there are over 300,000 wholesalers and over 1.6 million retailers. The entire distribution system in Japan is based on multi-layered networks with lots of wholesalers selling to other wholesalers.

The distribution strategy will also be closely tied to the pricing strategy employed. In countries with long distribution channels, price escalation through a large number of intermediaries – each of which will be adding margins – can be a major problem.

Channel decisions

One of the first decisions a company has to make when selecting intermediaries for international markets is, should direct or indirect channels be used? In other words, should they use indirect channels such as outside sales agents and distributors in the country, or should the product be distributed directly, using the company's sales force or company-owned distribution channel in a foreign country?

The former option is an independent channel, which is non-integrated and affords the producer in the home market very little or no control over international distribution and practically no links with the end users. On the other hand, direct distribution, which is an integrated channel, generally affords the manufacturer more control but, at the same time, brings responsibility, commitment and attendant risks.

Whether a company uses a direct channel or indirect channel can depend on a number of factors. One of these is the concentration of retailers in the market the company is developing its business in. In Germany, four retailers control 65% of the market. In operating in such a market, companies such as Richardsons Cutlery have decided to move from using indirect channels to having its own sales force. This has given it full control over managing the relationships with key customers. This is different to its operations in Italy, where no one retailer has more than 2% of the retail market. In such a market Richardsons Cutlery have used agents and local distributors with specialist local knowledge and local networks.

Over the last few years there has been increasing concentration of organisations in the forward supply chain – for example, fewer but much larger retailers. It has become increasingly important to select the most effective and appropriate distribution channel to move the product from the producer to the end customer. The appropriateness and effectiveness of the channel is dependent on the objectives of each of the channel members, their resources and the degree of influence within the channel.

As previously mentioned, there are many differences between distribution channels in different countries and the ideal channel may not be available in a particular country. In such situations the company has the dilemma of whether to modify its global marketing strategy and use existing channels or develop its own alternative distribution channel, which will prove costly.

In selecting appropriate channel intermediaries, a company has to consider many factors. Czinkota & Ronkainen (1988) suggested the 11C model to explain the factors a company should consider in their selection process. The eleven elements they suggest that need to be considered are:

- Customer characteristics.
- Culture, competition.
- Company objectives.
- Character of the market.
- Cost.
- Capital required.
- Coverage needed.
- Control issues.
- Continuity provided.
- Communication effectiveness.

Activity 14.1

Using the World Wide Web as the key research tool, for a product and international market of your choice try to identify agents who carry the specified product.

Examine the services they offer to foreign companies wishing to set up distribution systems in their country.

Management control in international distribution channels

In international marketing the distributor, agent or retailer is the main contact that an international customer has with the company located in its home market. This influences the customers' perception of the manufacturer's level of customer service. The implication of this is that the manufacturer or service provider has to ensure that the local channel members provide the desired level of service. This can be achieved by ensuring that they are adequately trained, receive and provide a free flow of market and product information and that their performance is continually monitored and evaluated.

Cultural differences across markets add to management and control difficulties. Typically, companies have less control over international channels than they have in their domestic market. The usual pattern of international involvement is to have a smaller market share and to use longer distribution channels – by using more layers of distribution intermediaries. Both of these factors reduce the power of the manufacturer. Less channel power usually results in less control over the other channel members and this can result in a conflict of interest, which must be sensitively managed.

The process of managing such relationships is difficult. In some instances, difficulties may arise for legal reasons as in the case of the termination of an agency. In other situations they result when relationships have been initiated but not adequately nurtured. For example, the development of sales, through wholesalers and distributors, might be substantially influenced by past trading patterns and the expectation of future profitable sales, rather than based on a sound working knowledge of that intermediary.

Developing good working relationships

It is advisable to get to know an intermediary and establish good working relationships built on mutual trust and integrity before investing significantly in its services. Management problems are however greatly reduced if channel members are carefully selected and have carefully drafted contracts that have been mutually understood and agreed.

In ensuring a good relationship, companies find it important to ensure partners in the supply chain feel they are adequately rewarded for their services, that territorial guarantees are honoured and that the company fully supports marketing efforts in the country both in terms of financial and management resources. If this is achieved then the company has greater assurance that the expectation its international clientele may have, in terms of customer service, will be met.

Understanding the way in which the international customer perceives service is important. There will be considerable differences between their expectations and those of the domestic customer. Customers who are distant might be more concerned about the guarantees of reliable rapid availability than customers much closer to the production source. The ability to meet widely differing customer requirements in different countries needs to be effectively managed. In all countries, customers are becoming increasingly demanding. Managing the channel members involved in the international supply chain is, therefore, becoming significant in many sectors as supply chains become more integrated and retailers and members of the supply chain become more powerful.

Activity 14.2

Choose three or four of the countries in which a company you know of is active. Discuss with the company how the expectations of the customer in these countries vary and identify how this is reflected in their distribution strategy.

Trends and developments in distribution

The trends and developments in distribution in international markets are complex and numerous. In this section we will focus on three important developments and examine their impact on distribution in international markets. These are the emergence of Internet retailing, the globalisation of retailing and the trends in managing international logistics.

Internet retailing

Multi-media technology has provided a number of opportunities for interactive shopping which offer particular opportunities in international markets. Tele-shopping and the Internet offer suppliers the retailing opportunities for direct contact with consumers throughout the globe without the problems and expense of having to establish infrastructures in foreign country markets. This was discussed in the previous Session.

Globalisation of retailing

The French hypermarket groups, Carrefour and Promodes, the German discount food retailers Aldi and Lidl, the US retailer Wal-Mart and specialists Toys 'R' Us, and UK retailers such as Tesco and Staples are all actively pursuing global expansion strategies which are changing the face of international distribution.

The internationalisation of retailing has meant a new era of distribution is developing. This new competitive landscape in distribution has a number of implications for the development of the distribution strategies of international companies. The most important of these are:

- Power shifts in supply chains towards retailers.

- Intense concentrated competition with significant buyer power across country markets.

- Rapidly advancing technology, facilitating global sourcing and global electronic transactions.

- Unrelenting performance measures being demanded of suppliers by international retailers.

- Smart, informed, demanding consumers expecting high levels of customer service.

The intensive growth in the size and power of retailers means there is now tremendous pressure on suppliers to improve the quality of service to them. Retailers are demanding:

- Streamlined and flexible supply chains.

- Suppliers who can guarantee quality and reliability across global markets.

- The ability to supply high volumes and often intensive relationships with intermediaries in the supply chain.

- Suppliers who can meet the global sourcing requirements of large-scale retailers who wish to buy centrally across the globe.

International logistics

The internationalisation of retailers and intensified global competition in most industrial sectors has led to a downward pressure on costs in all companies. In servicing international markets a major cost is the logistical process the company uses to deliver its goods and services to these markets. In Europe, 75% of businesses operating across European markets have a pan-European logistics or distribution strategy in place. The logistics function is having an increasing influence in many parts of the business, especially in inventory planning, information technology, purchasing and manufacturing.

There are a number of factors influencing this change:

- Customers demanding improved levels of customer service.

- Electronic Data Interchange (EDI) becoming the all-pervading technology for companies to build links with customers, suppliers and distribution providers.

- Companies restructuring their physical distribution operations in response to the formation of regional trading blocs.

The restructuring of physical distribution in companies has spawned the phenomenon in the logistics sector of outsourcing which has extended to the whole range of other services now regarded as legitimate logistics tasks. Indeed, many of the multi-national logistics companies such as DHL, Fedex, UPS and TNT, the so called integrators, themselves outsource the functions they take on to small specialist suppliers.

Activity 14.3

Freight forwarders are playing an increasingly important role in international physical distribution. Discuss with the managers of an organisation of your choice as to how they use freight forwarders.

Write a short report advising them as to what other services such organisations can now offer.

Employing a company owned sales force

Companies with expansion plans and an interest in becoming more involved in global markets will eventually take control of implementing their own marketing strategies and establish and manage their own international sales force. This will be particularly important to a company when its marketing strategy requires a high level of service before or after the sale. A company's own sales force will be more likely to ensure that high levels of customer service are achieved.

Sometimes a company that has had a disappointing experience with an agent or distributor in a market may decide to set up its own sales force to ensure it has more control over its long-term development of the market. Following disappointing sales, Williamson Ltd, a company selling knives into the Italian market, decided to terminate the contract of their agent and set up their own, wholly owned sales force. The termination of the contract meant they were required to pay out heavy sums of compensation to the agent concerned. Even so, the company decided that in terms of its long-term strategic objectives in the market, this was a necessary expense.

A company can establish its own sales force in various forms, including: travelling export sales reps, domestic-based export department or division and foreign-based sales branch or subsidiary.

The advantages of using a company-owned sales force include:

- It provides far greater control over the sales and marketing effort since the sales force is now directly employed by the company.
- It facilitates formation of closer manufacturer-customer relationships.
- Once established, the company-owned sales force can be helpful in identifying and exploiting new international marketing opportunities.

The disadvantages of developing a company-owned sales force include:

- A relatively larger resource commitment.
- Somewhat higher exit costs, should the company decide to no longer serve a particular market.
- Increased exposure to unexpected changes in the political/social environment of the host country.

Setting up an overseas sales force

One common strategy is to begin direct export operations by establishing a domestic-based export department and/or using home-based travelling salespeople. Then, as sales reach a certain volume in the new market, the decision is made to set up a foreign-based sales branch or subsidiary in the country.

The new unit may be strictly a marketing/sales arm or may also involve a production or warehouse facility. In either event, the company must make a commitment of resources to develop its own direct sales force to sell the company's offerings and build relationships with the company's customers in that market.

It may well be that a company uses its own sales force for key accounts and agents and distributors for small accounts. Equally, its own sales force may work in conjunction with international intermediaries. Building links directly with customers but always with and through the intermediaries can be important if the company is not to jeopardise its relationships with its distribution partners in the markets concerned. This has the advantage of enabling the company to build relationships with the customer and the intermediaries whilst not having to make the capital investment required to run a wholly owned subsidiary.

Activity 14.4

List the various expectations your organisation has of its sales force.

What are the arguments for and against using a largely home country based sales force, a largely expatriate sales force, or host country nationals in your export markets to ensure these expectations are met?

Which approach does your company adopt and why?

Case Study – Playing the buying game

Anyone with the time to study the daily array of reports and predictions on the likely size of the e-business market in the years to come will have realised that selling things to Joe Public over the web, and other online media like interactive television, is only half the story. In fact, not even half. For business-to-business (b2b) e-commerce is set to dwarf the business-to-consumer (b2c) variety, which when you think about it is hardly surprising.

And if online retailers sell themselves to consumers on a promise of convenience in the b2b arena, there's more to it than that. 'E-procurement' brings significant benefits to businesses in reducing paperwork and administration, promoting 'in-contract' buying and offering buyers huge potential savings.

At a simple level, it may be a case of a supplier preparing an electronic catalogue to sit on the buyer's network. With the catalogue freely available to anyone authorised to access it, the buying process is simplified, and the incentive to buy out of contract, with the consequent loss of discounts negotiated between buyer and seller, is removed. And in the process, much of the time-consuming interaction between buyer and seller in the way of phone calls, faxes and hard copy orders is removed, saving time and streamlining the admin.

"People buying out of contract are buying more expensively," explains Richard Ingleton, corporate director at KPMG Consulting. "The reason people buy out of contract is because it is easier. But if the electronic catalogue is on your desktop and you can flick through it and place your order for the new PC or whatever you want and it will be delivered in the next couple of days, that easiness option is handled."

There's no shortage of examples of companies using e-procurement to save money. In the US, General Electric – total annual shopping bill: $35 billion – is using the electronic catalogue system on a grand scale to save millions of dollars each year. Supplier catalogues are posted on its Trading Partner Networks for buyers to check prices and buy online.

Other companies are holding electronic auctions for commodity products and indirect supplies such as furniture and stationery, giving prospective suppliers a bidding window of perhaps 48 hours to submit tenders for the supply of the goods.

1999 saw the emergence of 'metamediaries', who bring buyers and sellers of materials together, promising the buyers good deals on excess stock and the sellers a way of offloading said stock. It's a bit like lastminute.com for the steel business, or whatever industry the metamediary happens to operate in.

Early in the New Year in the United States, a dozen companies who you might have imagined already had sufficient buying power to be going on with, including Kellogg's, Bethlehem Steel and Prudential Insurance, came together to form a $17 billion Internet buying group.

In the UK, Sainsbury's Efficient Consumer Response (ECR) initiative uses an Internet-based system to share information between the retailer and its suppliers about the performance of promotions. Automating the information exchange in this way is allowing Sainsbury's and its suppliers to estimate required stock levels more accurately which, in the case of perishable goods, can bring about significant reduction in wastage.

You don't have to look too far to find other examples of how companies are using 'e-procurement' to simplify the buying process and save money. Just enter the word 'e-procurement' into a search engine yourself and get started. (Yahoo! for example returned 153,000 results – plenty to be going on with).

In the meantime, it's clear that there are significant benefits to be achieved through e-procurement, even if you don't quite have the buying power of General Electric. But as KPMG's Richard Ingleton explains, it does require conscious effort on both sides if the benefits are to be realised.

"The benefits are there for both buyers and sellers," says Ingleton, "but you've got to be in the market. You've got to provide the information and you've got to be willing to receive the information."

Source: *Marketing Business*, April 2000.

Questions

1. What are the benefits of e-procurement for organisations operating across borders?

2. What are the potential disadvantages for organisations operating across borders in losing the personal relationship between buyer and seller?

SUMMARY OF KEY POINTS

- In order to select appropriate international distribution and logistics strategies, organisations must gain knowledge of how distribution is organised in the overseas market.

- A key question to answer is, should direct or indirect channels be used?

- The 'longer' the channel and the more intermediaries involved, the more difficult it is for the home producer to maintain control over the service offered to the end user.

- Effective management of channel relationships is key to meeting customer service expectations.

- Careful selection of channel intermediaries bound by carefully drawn up and mutually agreed contracts is an essential part of sound channel management.

- Recent trends and developments in international distribution includes the use of EDI and outsourcing.

> - A home producer may develop a company owned sales force that sells directly to the customer or decide to use their sales force in conjunction with international intermediaries.

Improving and developing own learning

The following projects are designed to help you develop your knowledge and skills further by carrying out some research yourself. Feedback is not provided for this type of learning because there are no 'answers' to be found, but you may wish to discuss your findings with colleagues and fellow students.

Project A

Visit the web sites of some of the multi-national logistics companies such as DHL, Fedex, UPS and TNT to find out what services they offer their customers. Which of these might your organisation use? What are the reasons for your choice?

Project B

Read Paliwoda and Thomas, International Marketing, 3rd Edition, Chapter 7, Exhibit 7.4: Compaq's compact solution. Note how effective strategic decisions and management control measures have resulted in the organisation's ability to be more efficient, improve customer service and reduce costs.

Project C

Read Paliwoda and Thomas, International Marketing, 3rd Edition, Chapter 7, Exhibit 7.5: Distributor takes on parallel importers. What do you think of the strategy adopted by Borneo Motors to meet the challenge of parallel imports.

Feedback to activities

Activity 14.1

A company will look for a number of services in agents and in examining them they will be evaluating the strength of the agent with regard to their ability to deliver to meet agreed schedules, zero defect delivery, and their willingness to meet emergency needs, engage in Just in Time (JIT) delivery and hold inventory.

A useful starting point for this activity could be the web site of the government agency in your country that works to encourage exporters. In the UK this is www.tradepartners.gov.uk. Alternatively your local Chamber of Commerce and Industry may be helpful.

Activity 14.2

In attempting this activity you may wish to see how the channels used in each country vary in terms of:

- Why expectations vary.
- The structure and length of the supply chain in a country.
- The service consumers receive.
- The feedback systems put in place by the company.
- The level of communication it receives from its supply chain partners?

Activity 14.3

Freight forwarders provide a wide range of services including:

- Preparation and processing of international transport documents.
- Co-ordination of transport services.
- Provision of warehousing.
- Expert advice.

Nowadays, the activities of freight forwarders usually include ownership of domestic and international road transport.

The opening of the channel tunnel, the widening membership of the European Union, advances in information technology and a greater number of worldwide business transactions have all contributed to freight forwarders playing a much greater role in the logistics management for companies in their international markets.

Activity 14.4

In listing the expectations of your company consider expectations with regard to:

- Product knowledge.

- Empathy with customers.

- Provision of feedback on the product or service.

These then need to be considered with reference to the advantages and disadvantages of using a company owned sales force outlined in the Session text.

Session 15

Implementing international marketing strategy

Introduction

Earlier Sessions have discussed the individual elements of international marketing strategy implementation, so in this final Session we look at the strategic issues associated with integrating these elements. We will consider the issues that must be addressed in individual country plans and evaluation and monitoring to ensure that implementation goes according to the plan. Finally, we look at the problems that arise because the strategy is implemented at different rates in different countries, due to local conditions.

LEARNING OUTCOMES

At the end of this Session you will be able to:

- Describe how an international marketing strategy may be implemented across different countries.

- Discuss the relevant tactical/operational issues when implementing an international marketing strategy across different countries.

- Establish criteria for control and evaluation of marketing and other business functions.

- Discuss the strategic implications of different rates of implementation across the developed and developing world.

Elements of implementation

The elements of implementation might be considered as follows:

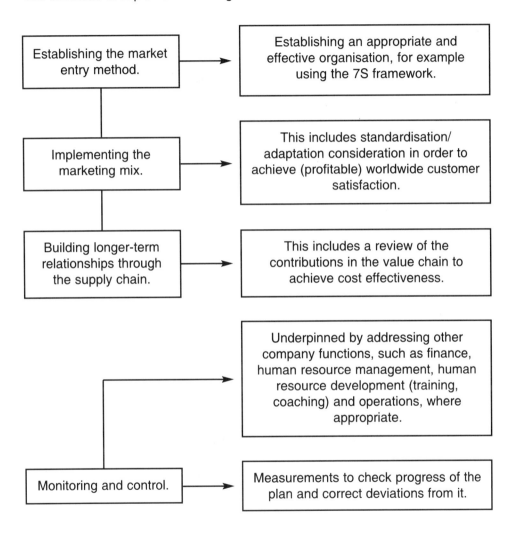

Figure 15.1: Elements of implementation

Perhaps the key decision in implementing the company's strategy is establishing an appropriate country presence. As we have discussed earlier, this involves deciding upon the level of involvement that is desirable or allowed in different markets. If the company finds it necessary or desirable to operate different market entry strategies, then it becomes more difficult to maintain consistent standards and values in the external relationships that are formed and the internal management culture that develops. For example, will managers working in a joint venture in one country and for a wholly owned subsidiary in another have exactly the same objectives, commitment and ways of working?

Marketing mix decisions will vary in emphasis in different country operations and there is a balance to be struck between making changes to the marketing mix because of the demands of local country managers ('this country is different because...') and the desire of the organisation to standardise its programmes and processes. In contrast some companies do allow considerable autonomy to the individual country managers to implement the strategy.

A key issue centres on building and managing relationships in the supply chain, particularly for multinational companies. They must decide the degree to which the responsibility for this should be undertaken by local country managers working in the interests of the local operation, local managers wearing their 'multinational hat' and taking responsibility on behalf of the worldwide organisation, or whether responsibility should be left to headquarters staff.

The international marketing strategy implementation requires support from other business functions and key decisions include:

- How the local country operations are financed, and the priority given to local investment.
- How to manage human resources, and the authority and autonomy that the local country has to make decisions on staff recruitment, reward, promotion, training and development.
- The degree of autonomy given to operations management.

Effective monitoring and control not only measure progress being made but also enable comparisons to be made between country operations.

Activity 15.1

Prepare a PowerPoint presentation entitled 'The challenges of implementing an international marketing strategy across different countries'.

Think global – act local again!

Underpinning local tactical implementation is the now very familiar slogan 'think global – act local'. All through this Companion we have stressed the problem of finding an appropriate balance between standardisation and adaptation. We have seen how environmental, competition and customer factors can create barriers to standardising the analysis, strategy development, and the marketing mix in all countries. At a local level, country managers will view their own set of circumstances as unique within the company. Head office, by contrast, will view individual country problems as largely local inconveniences in driving through the global marketing strategy and delivering the corporate objectives.

Issues in implementation

Implementation of strategy across different countries can be considered under three headings:

- International marketing programmes.
- International marketing processes.
- Organisational development.

By programmes we mean largely the marketing mix. For example, a company might wish to relaunch its corporate identity, carry out a rebranding exercise, develop a new product that will be suitable for a global market, undertake a pan regional advertising campaign, or plan a pan regional new product launch programme. Dealing with the need to adapt because of local country differences due to culture, usage and local laws means that modifications will inevitably have to be made.

The idea of a global or pan-regional advertising campaign implies a standardised brand, common creative work and so on but usually this is not appropriate. The name Toyota had to be created because the previous brand name only worked in local markets and could not be transferred to international markets. 'Diet' in China is translated as strictly bread and water and in France diet is related very directly to health, so the term 'Lite' is used for products such as Coca-Cola in those countries.

A pan-promotion strategy by Shell to band together anti-freeze and de-icer for cars for a winter campaign throughout Europe had to exclude Greece!

By contrast, processes are perhaps less culturally sensitive in that the elements of a process can be the same, but the way in which the elements are carried out and the results are obtained may be different. So, by processes we mean, for example, the marketing information or research process, the international marketing planning process, the new product development process and the monitoring and control process.

For companies in global consultancy, such as Deloitte and Touche and Accenture, and legal practice, such as Linklatter, each piece of work will differ in content, but a standardised process is essential for generating and analysing data, delivering solutions, promoting the company and its services, calculating costs and carrying out the work efficiently.

A process might be helpful, for example, for addressing the fact that managers pay insufficient attention to evaluating specific marketing programmes. So, for example, processes might be set up to improve:

- The success of investment decisions, in order to better decide between investing in product development, new market development and improving the efficiency of operations.

- Individual customer segment profitability, in order to decide whether it is better to focus upon retaining or winning new customers.

- The effectiveness of different promotional programmes by measurement and sharing results.

A model that might be used to consider the organisational development issues to support implementation is the 7S framework, because it addresses some key management dimensions: Shared values, Strategy, Structure, Systems, management Style, Skills and Staff.

Activity 15.2

For your organisation, or one you know well, consider the challenges that are posed in standardising each of the three dimensions above by completing the following table:

	Evidence of where we have standardised	Evidence of where we have adapted
■ International marketing programmes		
■ International marketing processes		
■ Organisational development		

The purpose of monitoring and control

Building control into the strategy implementation plan is vital for a number of reasons:

- To set clear priorities and targets that will drive the actions of the business units and both motivate managers and bring them to account.

- To enable an assessment to be made of progress towards short and long-term objectives.

- To set points where decisions need to be made if things are not going to plan.

- To enable comparisons to be made of performance between individual country operations or between strategic business units.

- To encourage a more effective planning culture throughout the company, not just in areas that are familiar with routine and detailed planning.

By using clearly understood measurements control can be applied to operations in order to initiate an evaluation of the efficiency and effectiveness of the marketing, and other business functions both for individual operations and collectively for the company as a whole. For this reason there tends to be a hierarchy of indicators used and typically these are agreed in the formal planning process. For example:

- Corporate objectives and budgeting typically include financial performance indicators, such as return on investment, profit, cash flow and earnings per share.

- Local country operation indicators are commonly used such as sales, profit margins, and cash flow.

- Marketing objectives are measured via market share, product profit margins, brand awareness and level of complaints.

Good practice in this area focuses not just on control and measurement, but also on improving performance throughout the company by developing good practice. A number of alternative approaches for evaluation, control and improvement have been developed over the years to support both general management and specific marketing actions.

Performance improvement methods

Total Quality Management (TQM) was, perhaps, the first method but other variants and alternatives are now available. If you are not already familiar with TQM and the following techniques, you should read about them in more detail.

Benchmarking involves comparing the performance of a specific activity (for example, logistics) between different SBUs within the company, between the company and competitors or with the best in the class (not necessarily from your own industry). The key tasks are to determine the key performance indicators that will ultimately lead to improvements that will be valued by customers, compare performance and find ways of improving performance, before measuring again.

The balanced scorecard (Kaplan 1992) is used to assess all relevant areas of performance, and includes the customer, internal business, financial, innovation and learning perspectives of the company. The key to success is in the selection of measures that clearly reflect the company's objectives and strategies.

Self-assessment is the basis of the Business Excellence Model and takes the form of regular, systematic reviews of processes, use of human and other resources and results. The concept for this approach is that customer satisfaction, employee satisfaction and a positive impact on society lead to satisfactory business performance.

Underpinning all these techniques is the need to develop a learning organisation that develops good practice, shares new ideas and develops greater confidence in the abilities of its staff so that they can be empowered to take decisions in their own area of expertise and knowledge.

Activity 15.3

Choose an area of business unit activity where you believe you are underperforming.

Use either a flowchart or bullet points on one sheet of paper to explain how one of the above techniques could be used to improve performance.

The reasons for differing rates of implementation

As companies assess the progress that has been made in implementing plans across their worldwide markets, it will become apparent that comparative performance will vary considerably. These differences will be explained in many cases by:

- Environmental factors, including the country's stage of development, customers' ability to pay and poor country infrastructure.

- Market factors, including poor distribution and retailing, low-priced local competition.

- Company factors, such as having a small-scale operation with very limited resources, often operated by inexperienced managers and staff with limited skills.

- Product factors, including an inappropriate product range, inadequate supply chain of components and services.

However, frequently there will be other reasons too, including a poorer understanding of customers and their needs, lack of cultural empathy and, sometimes, previous actions that might have alienated some customers. These factors may be very significant but are harder to identify and correct.

Differences in performance also occur between developed markets that might be judged to offer the same degree of potential revenue generation. The reasons for this could well include a number of the above factors but also aggressive actions by multinational competitors in individual markets.

The implications of differing rates of implementation

In some business sectors that are not particularly global in nature, different implementation rates may not cause a problem. The company might adopt a strategy that is essentially multi-domestic in nature and allow considerable local autonomy. Products and services can be at different stages of the international product life cycle and other marketing mix activity can respond to local factors.

By contrast different implementation rates can be problematic in sectors that are more global in nature. High technology companies that have invested heavily in new products must achieve rapid implementation of their plans to survive and grow. Producers of fast moving consumer goods that wish to develop a reputation for marketing leading edge products around the world must achieve consistency in implementation.

Success and failure

Because of uncontrollable environmental factors or poor performance by a subsidiary company or its managers, there are many examples of success and failure in individual country markets. Sometimes underperformance goes against a general trend in the company and surprises the management. Despite significant investment in South Africa, Pepsi-Cola was forced to pull out of the country in 1997 because its performance was so poor.

Many retailers have under-performed in foreign countries and have withdrawn from markets after investing heavily – for example Marks & Spencer in France. Such withdrawals not only affect company performance but can also seriously affect the company's image and morale, too.

Equally, innovation, an effective business model and weak competition can lead to surprising success. This has helped Müller to dominate the yoghurt market in the UK.

Case Study – Globally led, locally driven

At the Marketing Forum (1999) there was a session by Mike Moran, marketing director for Toyota (UK) called 'Anyone chasing the Holy Grail of an ad which will appeal to a Brit, a German and a Frenchman is a jerk'. Perhaps he's right. We've all seen examples of badly dubbed ads that land on our TV screens making a joke that appeals in the brand's homeland and nowhere else. Lufthansa's laughing crew campaign of a couple of years ago comes to mind. As does Grecian 2000 and Ferrero Rocher, which have been "really spoiling us" with their attempts at pan-European campaigns. Yet despite this, huge brands like Levi's and Coca-Cola continue with marketing initiatives and advertising that span many borders. So what should marketers who have responsibilities beyond one country do?

Arguments against global campaigns start with the fact that consumer behaviour is fundamentally different between cultures. For example, the French eat four times as much yoghurt as the British, and the British eat eight times more chocolate than the Italians. And if you're in the business of selling hot chocolate one campaign won't do. In South America, hot chocolate is a revitalising drink to have at breakfast and start the day, whereas in the UK it's a comfort drink to have just before going to bed. Perhaps differences like these are why so many cases of forced local adoption fail. Overall, there is a danger of ignoring important differences between nations and cultures, limiting imagination and producing ads to a lowest common denominator.

Cultural differences can also be a problem when targeting an individual country with many inherent diversities. India, for example, contains many ethnic and religious groups and languages.

Legal restrictions on advertising can have a major bearing on creativity and strategy. In Italy, levels of nudity in advertising are accepted that would be banned in some other countries.

Brands and markets are also often at different stages of development in different countries and held in different levels of esteem. Levi's jeans in the US are regarded as a staple product, but in Europe – despite the company's recent problems in 2000 – it remains a premium brand. There's evidence that US brands sell better in countries that are culturally similar. No surprise then that Canada and the UK are America's strongest export destinations. This sits against a commonly held view that US products enjoy "universal presence and cultural acceptance" (Levitt). The upshot is that in some cases global marketing initiatives experience diminishing returns.

Standardisation of marketing – particularly of advertising – implies a high degree of standardisation of actual product. Therefore, lower costs derived from greater production volumes and reduced changes in factory set-ups could lead to competitive advantage.

Standardisation may also mean that lower advertising costs can be achieved. If the same advertising execution can be used across borders then potentially millions can be saved on expensive advertising production costs.

Brand power and scope affect customer choices and presenting a standard brand image across countries may communicate the brand's credibility. Its wide availability as observed by a largely mobile population in, for example, Europe may indicate high quality and convenience for consumers. Look at Avis which delivers its "we try harder" promise very consistently. Consistency in brand image is important in a world where media transmits images across borders. One of the best examples of a brand that communicates functional superiority worldwide is Gillette Sensor.

The landscape for global brands is changing fast, particularly in relation to youth markets, thanks to increased consumer mobility, better communication capabilities and expanding transnational entertainment options.

Cultural experiences are increasingly shared. A compelling argument in youth markets is that teenagers in London, Rome, Berlin and Tel Aviv have more in common with each other than they do with their parents. Fashion, music, the Internet and football are creating a homogeneous youth culture and 'culture-bound products' are emerging that are targeted at, for example, 18-25 year old males across the world. A global demography is emerging that makes consistent marketing across borders not only desirable but essential. The emergence of relationships as a way to think about marketing intuitively fits with a young audience influenced by an emerging 'world-culture' based on empathy. Conventional 'Cartesian' research may not reveal important details about how people buy, so the development of an advertising language more in tune with how people choose is needed.

Standardising the advertising strategy is just one element of marketing practice that simplifies co-ordination and provides greater control over the brand's presentation. Good marketing ideas are hard to find, so exploiting them across borders is a benefit. Advertising will help maintain sales, but only building brand equity will increase them.

So there are some strong arguments against marketing standardisation across borders, but some strong compelling arguments why in certain markets, failing to standardise seems at best wasteful and at worst a way to destroy shareholder value. So what's the best approach?

Keith Kirby, MD of Elmwood worked with Orange for six years from the creation of the brand through to helping introduce it to a number of other countries. The lessons from that seem to strike the right balance between completely global, centrally dominated campaigns and fragmented local initiatives. The success comes down to two things: the passion of the people and a belief that the core brand values are universal themes. They might mean slightly different things to different people in different places but the values do not change across borders. Orange's challenge was to find where to turn the volume up and down on the values for maximum impact in each market. For example, in Israel, it was discovered that stressing honesty only led people to believe that you had something to hide. The UK experience was used to test the water in each market, but it was felt wrong to import the UL communications brand en masse.

So we worked with the local operating companies and their local agencies, firstly to explain the Orange brand essence – the brand DNA that should be present in everything the brand touches – and then secondly to help shape the creative brief. You might think such an approach would be met with local hostility , but on the contrary, an open and unthreatening discussion emerged and the local agencies became very keen to get it right for Orange as well as right for their market. Today, if you look at the way the brand is interpreted in the local markets you can find a strong link that is made by the brand DNA, but in each case there is a local characteristic too.

If you're working in the EU for example, and appealing to customers across borders, try looking for themes that are universally appealing to young Europeans, the key similarities, and avoid being distracted by the differences. Be sensitive to local needs but look how your brand's DNA can work for those needs and produce the best result for your brand and the local market.

Source: *Marketing Business*, May 2000.

Questions

1. Why is the landscape for global brands changing, particularly for youth markets?

2. Why is it so important to be aware of local market needs when introducing a product to an overseas market?

3. What might be the consequences for organisations that fail to find a way to match local needs and brand DNA?

SUMMARY OF KEY POINTS

- The elements of implementation are establishing market entry method, improving and adapting marketing mix, building long-term relationships throughout the supply chain and putting in place effective means of monitoring and control.

- Effective monitoring and control may include the use of performance improvement techniques such as TQM, Benchmarking, Balanced Scorecard and Business Excellence Model.

- Differing rates of strategy implementation may be due to environmental, market, company and/or product factors.

- The ultimate penalty for ineffective strategy implementation is failure and damage to reputation.

Improving and developing own learning

The following projects are designed to help you develop your knowledge and skills further by carrying out some research yourself. Feedback is not provided for this type of learning because there are no 'answers' to be found, but you may wish to discuss your findings with colleagues and fellow students.

Project A

Read Usunier, 2000, *Marketing Across Cultures*, 3rd Edition, Chapter 8, Case: Lakewood Forest Products (page 274) and answer the questions set.

Project B

Read Usunier, 2000, *Marketing Across Cultures*, 3rd Edition, Chapter 12, Case: Aunt Sarah's Fried Chicken (page 407) and answer the questions set.

Project C

Identify one country in which your organisation is underperforming, compared to what might be expected. Identify the reasons.

In carrying out this activity pay particular attention to the different areas such as:

- Environmental factors (SLEPT).
- Market factors (competition, supply chain problems).
- Company factors (management, structure, staff, skills etc.).
- Cultural factors (mismatch with your products).

Feedback to activities

Activity 15.1

Use bullet points to identify the key issues in:

- Determining the market entry method.
- Marketing mix programmes and processes.
- Building the local organisation.
- Effective monitoring and control.

Activity 15.2

Having carried out this activity you should think about:

- Where opportunities for standardisation still exist and what the benefits will be.
- Where standardisation would be too restrictive.
- How appropriate the organisation's approach is.

Activity 15.3

To achieve process improvement it is important to obtain 'buy-in' from all staff by involving them in the process. This requires a clear explanation of:

- The benefits (not only for the organisation but also to help staff to do their job better).

- The fact that these processes are based on co-operation (not blame).

- Management and feedback should be constructive, looking for improvements rather than only applying controls.

Glossary

Glossary

Above-the-line – advertising for which a payment is made and for which a commission is paid to the advertising agency.

Account management – the process by which an agency or supplier manages the needs of a client.

ACORN (A Classification of Residential Neighbourhoods) – a database which divides up the entire population of the UK in terms of housing in which they live.

Added value – the increase in worth of a product or service as a result of a particular activity – in the context of marketing this might be packaging or branding.

Advertising – promotion of a product, service or message by an identified sponsor using paid-for media.

AIDA (Attention, Interest, Desire, Action) – a model describing the process that advertising or promotion is intended to initiate in the mind of a prospective customer.

Ansoff Matrix – model relating marketing strategy to general strategic direction. It maps product/market strategies.

BCG Matrix – model for product portfolio analysis.

Below-the-line – non-media advertising or promotion when no commission has been paid to the advertising agency.

Brand – the set of physical attributes of a product or service, together with the beliefs and expectations surrounding it.

Business plan – a strategic document showing cash flow, forecasts and direction of a company.

Business strategy – the means by which a business works towards achieving its stated aims.

Business to business (b2b) – relating to the sale of a product for any use other than personal consumption.

Business to consumer (b2c) – relating to the sale of a product for personal consumption.

Buying behaviour – the process that buyers go through when deciding whether or not to purchase goods or services.

Channels – the methods used by a company to communicate and interact with its customers.

Comparative advertising – advertising which compares a company's product with that of competing brands.

Competitive advantage – the product, proposition or benefit that puts a company ahead of its competitors.

Confusion marketing – controversial strategy of deliberately confusing the customer.

Consumer – individual who buys and uses a product or service.

Consumer behaviour – the buying habits and patterns of consumers in the acquisition and usage of products and services.

Copyright – the law that protects the originator's material from unauthorised use, usually (in the UK) for seventy years after the originator's death.

Corporate identity – the character a company seeks to establish for itself in the mind of the public.

Corporate reputation – a complex mix of characteristics such as ethos, identity and image that go to make up a company's public personality.

Culture – a shared set of values, beliefs and traditions that influence prevailing behaviour within a country or organisation.

Customer – a person or company who purchases goods or services.

Customer loyalty – feelings or attitudes that incline a customer to return to a company, shop or outlet to purchase there again.

Customer Relationship Management (CRM) – the coherent management of contacts and interactions with customers.

Customer satisfaction – the provision of goods or services which fulfil the customer's expectations in terms of quality and service, in relation to price paid.

DAGMAR (Defining Advertising Goals for Measured Advertising Response) – a model for planning advertising in such a way that its success can be quantitatively monitored.

Data processing – the obtaining, recording and holding of information which can then be retrieved, used, disseminated or erased.

Data Protection Act – a law which makes organisations responsible for protecting the privacy of personal data.

Database marketing – whereby customer information stored in an electronic database is utilised for targeting marketing activities.

Decision Making Unit (DMU) – the team of people in an organisation or family group who make the final buying decision.

Demographic data – information describing and segmenting a population in terms of age, sex, income and so on which can be used to target marketing campaigns.

Differentiation – ensuring that products and services have a unique element to allow them to stand out from the rest.

Direct mail – delivery of an advertising or promotional message to customers or potential customers by mail.

Direct marketing – all activities that make it possible to offer goods or services or to transmit other messages to a segment of the population by post, telephone, email or other direct means.

Direct Response Advertising – advertising incorporating a contact method such as a phone number or enquiry form with the intention of encouraging the recipient to respond directly to the advertiser.

Distribution (Place) – the process of getting the goods from the manufacturer or supplier to the user.

Diversification – an increase in the variety of goods and services produced by an organisation.

E-commerce – business conducted electronically.

E-marketing – marketing conducted electronically.

Electronic Point of Sale (EPOS) – a system whereby electronic tills are used to process customer transactions in a retail outlet.

Ethical marketing – marketing that takes account of the moral aspects of decisions.

Export marketing – the marketing of goods or services to overseas customers.

Field marketing – extending an organisation's marketing in the field through merchandising, product launches, training of retail staff, etc.

FMCG (Fast Moving Consumer Goods) – such as packages of food and toiletries.

Focus groups – a tool for marketing research where small groups of participants take part in guided discussions on the topic being researched.

Forecasting – calculation of future events and performance.

Franchising – the selling of a licence by the owner (franchisor) to a third party (franchisee) permitting the sale of a product or service for a specified period.

Geo-demographics – a method of analysis combining geographic and demographic variables.

Grey market (silver market) – term used to define a population over a certain age (usually 65).

Industrial marketing (or business to business marketing) – the marketing of industrial products.

Innovation – development of new products, services or ways of working.

Internal customers – employees within an organisation viewed as 'consumers' of a product or service provided by another part of the organisation.

Internal marketing – the process of eliciting support for a company and its activities among its own employees in order to encourage them to promote its goals.

International marketing – the conduct and co-ordination of marketing activities in more than one country.

Key account management – account management as applied to a company's most valuable customers.

Logo – a graphic usually consisting of a symbol and or group of letters that identifies a company or brand.

Macro environment – the external factors which affect companies' planning and performance, and are beyond its control. (SLEPT).

Market development – the process of growing sales by offering existing products (or new versions of them) to new customer groups.

Market penetration – the attempt to grow one's business by obtaining a larger market share in an existing market.

Market research – the gathering and analysis of data relating to markets to inform decision making.

Marketing research – the gathering and analysis of data relating to marketing to inform decision making (includes product research, place research, pricing research, etc.).

Market segmentation – the division of the marketplace into distinct sub-groups or segments, each characterised by particular tastes and requiring a specific marketing mix.

Market share – a company's sales of a given product or set of products to a given set of customers expressed as a percentage of total sales of all such products to such customers.

Marketing audit – scrutiny of an organisation's existing marketing system to ascertain its strengths and weaknesses.

Marketing communications (Promotion) – all methods used by a firm to communicate with its customers and stakeholders.

Marketing information – any information used or required to support marketing decisions.

Marketing mix – the combination of marketing inputs that affect customer motivation and behaviour (7 Ps – Product, Price, Promotion, Place, People, Process and Physical Evidence).

Marketing orientation – a business strategy whereby customers' needs and wants determine corporate direction.

Marketing planning – the selection and scheduling of activities to support the company's chosen marketing strategy or goals.

Marketing strategy – the broad methods chosen to achieve marketing objectives.

Micro environment – the immediate context of a company's operations, including such elements as suppliers, customers and competitors.

Mission statement – a company's summary of business philosophy, purpose and direction.

Model – simplified representation of a process, designed to aid in understanding.

New Product Development (NPD) – the creation of new products from evaluation of proposals through to launch.

Niche marketing – the marketing of a product to a small and well-defined segment of the marketplace.

Objectives – a company's defined and measurable aims or goals for a given period.

Packaging – material used to protect and promote goods.

Personal selling – one-to-one communication between seller and prospective purchaser.

PIMS (Profit Impact of Marketing Strategies) – a US database supplying data such as environment, strategy, competition and internal data.

Porter's Five Forces – an analytic model developed by Michael E. Porter which analyses the competitive environment and industry structure.

Positioning – the creation of an image for a product or service in the minds of customers, both specifically to that item and in relation to competitive offerings.

Product life cycle – a model describing the progress of a product from the inception of the idea through the peak of sales, to its decline.

Promotional mix – the components of an individual campaign which are likely to include advertising, personal selling, public relations, direct marketing, packaging and sales promotion.

Public Relations (PR) – the planned and sustained communication to promote mutual understanding between an organisation and its stakeholders.

Pull promotion – addresses the customer directly with a view to getting them to demand the product and hence 'pull' it down through the distribution chain.

Push promotion – relies on the next link in the distribution chain, e.g. wholesaler, to 'push' out products to the customer.

Qualitative research – information that cannot be measured or expressed in numeric terms. It is useful to the marketer as it often explores people's feelings and opinions.

Quantitative research – information that can be measured in numeric terms and analysed statistically.

Reference group – a group with which the customer identifies in some way and whose opinions and experiences influence the customer's behaviour.

Relationship marketing – the strategy of establishing a relationship with a customer which continues well beyond the first purchase.

Return on investment – the value that an organisation derives from investing in a project.

Sales promotion – a range of techniques used to increase sales in the short term.

Skimming – setting the original price high in the early stages of the product life cycle to get as much profit as possible before prices are driven down by increasing competition.

SLEPT – a framework for viewing the macro environment – Socio-cultural, Legal, Economic, Political and Technical factors.

SMART – a mnemonic referring to the need for objectives to be Specific, Measurable, Achievable, Relevant and Timebound.

Sponsorship – specialised form of promotion where a company will help fund an event or support a business venture in return for publicity.

Stakeholder – an individual or group that affects or is affected by the organisation and its operations.

Supplier – an organisation or individual that supplies goods or services to a company.

Targeting – the use of market segmentation to select and address a key group of potential purchasers.

Unique Selling Proposition (USP) – the benefit that a product or service can deliver to customers that is not offered by any competitor.

Vision – the long-term aims and aspirations of the company for itself.

Word-of-mouth – the spreading of information through human interaction alone.

Appendix 1

Feedback to Case Studies

Session 1   Zimflowers

1. Choose either other European or ASEAN countries as possible new market destinations.

    Outline the factors which the Horticultural Promotion Council should consider before entering the market.

    - Make sure you choose a particular market in a specified region, then for that market consider:
    - Internal factors to Zimflowers.
    - Internal factor relevant to Zimbabwe(government help, investment assistance etc.).
    - PEST analysis.
    - 12C analysis.
    - Supply chain factors (e.g. power of buyers, branding issues, relationships etc.).
    - Market mix factors (e.g. differentiation required, promotion price setting issues).

Session 2   Zack and Justin's

1. As a Marketing Consultant advising the board of Zack and Justin's, analyse all the strategic options (specifically international) open to the company. What factors should the company take into account in evaluating these?

    - International entry options: sell out, strategic partnerships/alliances, franchise, joint venture.
    - Advantages (financial gain, staying in the business).
    - Disadvantages (local opinion, possible rationalisation, loss of company culture and standards.
    - Ethical issues.

2. Based on this evaluation, what advice would you give the company?

    - Cause issues.

- Realistic low budget campaign.
- Message to international audience.
- Use of Media, PR, international celebrity.
- Campaign to resist international acquisition.

Session 3   Car wars

As a Marketing Consultant to a small volume (200,000 units per annum) car manufacturer of medium priced cars which exports mainly to the UK (20% of production) advise on the possible effects on the company of the shifts in global car manufacturing and marketing as described in the case.

- One market in a globalised industry.
- Impact of PEST customer, market restructure and competition factors.
- Effect on domestic economy and international stakeholders.
- Difficulty of planning without country presence.

Session 4   Branching out

1. What might be the short- and long-term effects for a company, in its domestic market and internationally, that inadvertently offended national pride or dignity by using an inappropriate colour in its packaging?

    Short term:

    - Consumer loss of confidence.
    - Brand boycotting.
    - Inappropriate brand positioning.

    Long term:

    - Whispering campaign against the brand may take a long time to quell.
    - Difficult for any subsequent launch to dispel the initial bad impact.

2. What might be the benefits and disadvantages for rights owners using a 'one stop shop' for their European licensing programmes?

    - Easier to ensure EU rules and directives complied with.
    - Economies of scale in distributions.
    - Easier control of stock and servicing of client orders.
    - Pan-euro advertising campaign.

■ Builds the capacity to compete against other global and pan-euro licensing programmes.

Session 5   Knowledge Interact Ltd

1. As a consultant contracted to Knowledge Interact Ltd., provide advice to the Board on the types of market information which it would require to aid the decision on where to locate its new headquarters.

    ■ Environmental information – PEST data.
    ■ Infrastructure analysis.
    ■ Market potential information.
    ■ 12C analysis.
    ■ State of location development.

2. What type of information does it need to decide online services would it offer to potential web site marketers?

    ■ Location of potential clients.
    ■ Size type of potential clients and their businesses.
    ■ Type of services required.
    ■ Amount of money prepared to pay for services.
    ■ Competitive offerings in the potential services.
    ■ Degree of access to the right technology.
    ■ Technological infrastructure.

Session 6   INDECO (PVT) Ltd

Assume that the decision has been taken for INDECO to enter the Zambian market again.

As the Marketing Analyst write an International Strategic Marketing Plan for the Board, covering the years 2002-2004, based around one direct market entry of your choice.

■ Analysis:
  This should include a detailed market analysis and audit of the market using either the 12C framework or the Terpstra market profile analysis.

■ Planning:
  This should include a detailed three marketing strategy and marketing mix developed in line with the analysis and the difficulties and challenges

identified. It should include objective setting, short and long term.

■ Implementation and control issues in such a difficult market:
   – Selection of strategic focus.
   – Market entry strategy.
   – Selection of 7P mix.
   – Budgets.

Session 7   Reputation matters

1.   What evidence is there in the Case Study that Microsoft is a global thinker?

   ■ Conflicting: US centric driven, belated country responsiveness.

   ■ Previously concerned with exploiting competitive advantage.

   ■ Now recognising the need to be a good corporate citizen and be part of the wider community (SMEs, charities etc.).

2.   How has it structured the company to operate as a global organisation?

   ■ Centralised in response to areas of business challenge.

   ■ To deliver to technology oriented consumers.

   ■ Now trying to address poor country co-ordination of marketing implementation through decentralisation.

Session 8   Europe's attitude to the Net

1.   If national culture is reflected in organisational attitudes, what are the implications for international marketers of different attitudes to the Internet in different countries?

   ■ Examine how national culture is reflected in organisational attitudes.

   ■ Hofstede dimensions: uncertainty avoidance, power distance, level of individualism v collectivism and cultures values; feminine v masculine.

   ■ Apply each of these to e-business or Internet communication.

   ■ For example: in cultures where high levels of uncertainty avoidance may be slow to buy from Internet based suppliers.

2.   What impact would increasing consumer confidence in security for financial transactions on the Internet have on global reach for international companies?

- Expansion of products being sold over the Internet.
- Greater speed of market diffusion.
- Removal of geographical barriers to international expansion.
- Development of globally based home shopping.
- Much easier to develop integrated supply chain management systems to manage customer relations globally.

Session 9   Let the battle commence

1. What opportunities and threats exist for the British PO?

- Larger market and increased profits – economies of scale and the experience effect.
- Aggressive competition in the PO's British market and a decline in business.
- Under-investment and excessive bureaucratic control.

2. What competitive strategies could the British Post Office employ against Deutsche Post and other competition in the event that their monopoly is broken?

- Formation of alliances, joint ventures (possibly including with Deutsche Post).
- Niche marketing – selection of profitable segments.

Session 10 Levi Strauss

1. What environmental factors contributed to the 1998 position of Levi's?

- Changes in consumer taste.
- Changes in economics.
- Emergence of a fragmented market.
- Development of more competitive landscape internationally.
- Growing power of global ethical groups.

2. As a marketing consultant, what would you advise them to do in the three years following the article (1999-2002)? Give reasons for your answer.

- Build brand value.
- Tackle brand confusion.

- Defend against competitors by strategy development rather than seeking protection in courts.

- New competitive landscape requires new segmentation and new targeting strategy.

- Make changes in planning implementation and control cycle.

Session 11 A question of choice

1. As a marketing consultant what pricing strategy would you advise Levi's to adopt in the UK following the judgement?

Levi's are using the courts to protect their brand rather than brand investment. The value of their brand in the UK has deteriorated, not because of supermarkets like Tesco, but because they are failing in the competitive battle against other more fashionable jeans suppliers. In developing a pricing strategy for the UK, Levi's need to focus on the real competition and develop a pricing strategy to compete against them, rather than being hung up on the perception of their brand in supermarkets.

However, whilst the question asks you to consider the UK in isolation, it is a mistake to think that Levi's can operate in this way. Their pricing policy for the UK needs to be in line with that of other EU countries.

2. As consumers become more mobile, globally, how do you think brands need to adapt their pricing strategies. Give reasons for your answer.

Global brands need a global pricing policy. To achieve this, Levi's need to rethink their basis for segmenting international markets and need to rethink the platform on which they are building their brand. Many of the problems experienced by Levi's are due to that fact they are still segmenting on geographical lines and trying to have different pricing strategies for different geographical markets. However, as these markets can no longer be kept separate they can no longer sustain a differentiated pricing policy.

Session 12 Looking on the bright side

1. What advice does the Case Study give to advertisers contemplating launching a campaign in the East?

- Take care to be sensitive to cultural differences.

- Mistakes in language can cause offence and render a campaign a failure.

- That it is sometimes difficult to detect the differences in the nuances of language, as the same words have different connotations.

2. Why do you think the differences discussed 'run so deep'?

- Language key component of culture. Culture is ingrained and enduring and so only slowly changes over time.

- Language is based on the values shared within in a society. These are the indicators we use to make assessments so very important to understand. The consequence of not understanding them can be severe.

- Language is learned from a very early age and the values with it are learned from a very early age, and therefore it is difficult for people to unlearn what they have accepted all their lives.

3. How could you ensure that your advertising campaign is culturally acceptable for the market it is aimed at?

- Avoid Self Reference Criterion (SRC).

- Carry out a cultural sensitivity analysis for your product and markets.

- Involve local partners in developing your campaign.

- Do thorough piloting and testing of any advertising campaign in the market prior to launch.

Session 13 Marketing through reconciliation

1. What advice is given to organisations on achieving customer focus?

- Avoidance of self reference criterion.

- Necessity of understanding and recognising the implications of cultural nuances.

- The need for flexibility and adaptability in international markets.

- The importance of reconciling the differences opposing cultural viewpoints of the buyer and the seller.

2. What factors relating to consumer behaviour identified in the Case Study might you, as a marketer, need to consider if pursuing a policy of relationship marketing in a multinational enterprise?

- Impact of culture on negotiations, setting up of meetings and dealing with customers.

- The fact the West has a highly individualistic cultural heritage and the East is based more clearly on the family. This model is relevant in b2b as well as b2c marketing.

- Differences in the way consumers go through the consumer buying process. Most US consumer behaviour models assume a linear and rationale decision making process. The applicability of this to a number of cultures needs to be questioned.

Session 14 Playing the buying game

1. What are the benefits of e-procurement for organisations operating across borders?

   - Time to access product or service.
   - Already negotiated discount for quantity.
   - Instant access to information on products.
   - Real time quantitative information on product acceptance.

2. What are the potential disadvantages for organisations operating across borders in losing the personal relationship between buyer and seller?

   - Qualitative information on product acceptance.
   - Difficulty in negotiating tailor-made deals.
   - Less sensitivity to local market culture, conditions requirements.

Session 15 Globally led, locally driven

1. Why is the landscape for global brands changing, particularly for youth markets?

   - Increasing mobility of young people through travel.
   - Improved communication increasing awareness.
   - Homogenisation of their needs, wants, lifestyles and leisure interest.

2. Why is it so important to be aware of local market needs when introducing a product to an overseas market?

   - Products can fail due to one element (not necessarily core) of the augmented product and marketing support service not being acceptable.
   - Cultural insensitivity in designing the total product offer can lead to negative stakeholder response.

3. What might be the consequences for organisations that fail to find a way to match local needs and brand DNA?

    ■ Inappropriate strategies and implementation programmes (brand and marketing mix).

    ■ Inappropriate new product development.

    ■ Alienation of customers.

Appendix 2

Syllabus

International marketing strategy

Aims and objectives

- To develop a thorough understanding of international marketing theory and key concepts.

- To develop a knowledge and understanding of vocabulary associated with international/global marketing strategy in different types of economies, organisations and market situations.

- To appreciate the complexities of international and global marketing in a mix of economies.

- To create an awareness of processes, context and influences associated with international and global marketing strategies in a range of economies.

- To develop an appreciation of strategies and plans for a mix of international and global economies.

- To develop an understanding of the implications for implementation, monitoring and control of the international marketing planning process.

Learning outcomes

By the end of this module, you should be able to:

- Demonstrate an understanding of the changing nature of the international trading environment, the major trends, strategic and contextual, affecting the global decision and the different business and social/cultural conventions that affect buying behaviour.

- Determine marketing strategies appropriate to industrialised, developing and lesser developed economies and identify the relevant sources of information and analysis to support the appropriate strategy.

- Formulate strategies for export, international, multinational, transnational and global marketing operations and evaluate the relevant organisational changes as an organisation moves through the export to global spectrum.

- Select and justify an appropriate marketing strategy and evaluate the financial, human resource, operational and logistical implications of different strategies.

■ Determine the appropriate control measures in international operations.

Indicative content and weighting

2.1 International strategic analysis (30%)

2.1.1 Identifying and analysing opportunities in the international trading environment.

- ■ Changing patterns of trade globally and types of markets (product/service/commodity/not for profit).

2.1.2 The strategic and contextual elements of global operations – organisational and external. Global and multinational marketing as a strategic decision.

- ■ Strategic networking and the International supply chain.

2.1.3 The changes in the world-trading environment: Countries, world, regions (e.g. European Union ASEAN etc.) and trading blocs.

2.1.4 The SLEPT factors: Social/cultural, Legal, Economic, Political, Technological and ethical, green and other environmental considerations. The role and effect of pressure groups.

2.1.5 The "C" factors: Countries, currency, competitors and their effect on international marketing planning.

2.1.6 Evaluating customer buying behaviour (consumer, business, institutional) in different countries at different stages of economic and political development.

- ■ Using marketing research to identify opportunities, similarities and differences.

2.1.7 Market Research Agency selection for International marketing support, the use of databases, intelligent and expert systems. Government initiatives and the importance of cross-cultural analysis.

2.1.8 The use of competitive/absolute/comparative analysis in international market appraisal.

2.1.9 The consequences of a more ethical responsibility approach including green and environmental issues and their effect on global corporate operations.

2.2 International strategic planning (30%)

2.2.1 Different approaches to International Marketing Planning; Transactional; Relational, and knowledge based approaches between developed countries and Lesser Developed Countries (LSD's) and developing and emergent economies.

2.2.2 The organisational and management issues pertinent to the export to globalisation spectrum decision, organisational structures, cultures, capabilities and the leveraging of core competencies and capabilities.

2.2.3 The globalisation process-partnering, alliances, mergers and their effect on the structure of industry and the competitive environment.

2.2.4 The organisation as a learning organisation and non-linear approaches to planning, including expert and database system, emergent strategies and 'muddling through'.

2.2.5 The cross-cultural dimensions of global activity and cultural sensitivity.

2.2.6 The effect of market/economic transience on global operations and within the host country environment – social, supply chain, labour and economic factors.

2.2.7 Managing and controlling in-house and external resources. The expatriate, national and global staff.

2.2.8 Standardisation and differentiation: the issues of globalisation in international marketing.

2.2.9 The determination of market entry choices, selection and decision and the implications for strategy and sources of global finance to support entry strategies.

2.2.10 The determination of market entry choices, selection and decision and the implications for strategy.

2.2.11 Sources of global finance to support entry strategies.

2.3 International strategy implementation and control (40%)

2.3.1 Identifying and selecting a product management strategy.

2.3.2 Determining pricing strategies for International markets: Skimming and penetration pricing; currency considerations in exporting and international marketing. Price escalation in the value chain, the futures market, hedging/forward buying, tendering and bartering. The meaning and specifics of Incoterms and specific pricing methods.

2.3.3 Determining International marketing communications issues relating to international positioning strategies. The importance of cultural differences and similarities.

2.3.4 The selection of a distribution and logistics strategy. Foreign channel management. Channel members expectations and performance; customer service levels. The evolving forms of distribution, e.g. e-business.

2.3.5 Global technological developments and their strategic competitive effect e.g. e-commerce, Internet in general and global media.

2.3.6 The process and evidence of global operations – strategies, human and their physical transactional activities.

2.3.7 Assessing the people elements of global operations – cross/inter cultural dimensions and transaction activity and human involvement.

2.3.8 The role of a relationship marketing approach as complementary to a traditional marketing mix approach.

2.3.9 Implementing international/global marketing strategy across different countries and the strategic implications. The tactical and operational issues relevant to different countries and situations.

2.3.10 Establishing criteria for control and evaluation of marketing and other business functions including self-assessment, benchmarking, best practice, and the balanced scorecard. The strategic implications of differing rates of implementation across the developed and developing world.

Appendix 3

The Chartered
Institute of Marketing

Postgraduate Diploma in Marketing

International Marketing Strategy

9.52:   **International Marketing Strategy**

Time: **14.00-17.00**

Date: **5th December, 2001**

3 Hours Duration

This examination is in two sections.

PART A – Is compulsory and worth 40% of total marks.

PART B – Has **SIX** questions; select **THREE**. Each answer will be worth 20% of the total marks.

DO NOT repeat the question in your answer, but show clearly the number of the question attempted on the appropriate pages of the answer book.

Rough workings should be included in the answer book and ruled through after use.

© The Chartered Institute of Marketing

Postgraduate Diploma in Marketing

9.52:   International Marketing Strategy

PART A

Car Wars

"A decision in a Detroit Boardroom, 2,000 job losses in a Luton (UK) factory – the price we pay for globalisation".

This was the headline in the Financial Mail on Sunday Newspaper in December 2000. That year saw chaos looming in the UK car manufacturing and marketing scene.

Until the beginning of November 2000, there was not the slightest hint that the relatively efficient Vauxhall car factory at Luton, UK would close with the loss of 2,000 jobs. After all, it was only in 1998 that Vauxhall's Chairman and MD had given up his basic salary for a year in order to secure backing for a productivity linked pay deal designed to secure the future of car production at the plant. Yet the Vauxhall closure was not the only bad news to hit the industry. Despite having one of the most efficient car production plants in the world at Sunderland, in the North East of the UK, there was considerable speculation that Nissan was to move the new Micra production to France; however this has now been averted. Peugeot, the French car manufacturer, was warning that its £50 million investment in car manufacturing at Coventry, the traditional home of the UK car industry, was in the balance. BMW had already sold Rover. Ford had announced it was to end volume production at Dagenham, near London. Mercedes announced that at the end of year 2000 it was to close 40% of its dealers (from 156 to 63) threatening 2,000 jobs. Ford, Fiat and Volvo were all considering the future of their "independent" dealerships and working up a dedicated sales force deal in anticipation of a new EU ruling in 2003 which could end "manufacturers only" car dealerships. At the end of 2000, only Toyota offered a ray of hope. It had decided to produce a new model on the Derby production line instead of in France. At the end of year there was a great feeling that the industry has seen all this before.

In the 1960s, British manufacturers flourished but complacency, under-investment and poor labour relations, left the UK unprepared in the increasingly global marketplace of the 1970s, especially against growing competition from Asia Pacific and Europe. This all changed in the 1980s when government policy encouraged foreign inward investment as a means of entry into the larger European market. EU rules helped by limiting the number of Japanese imports. All looked rosy. So what went wrong? There were a number of factors. Many car manufacturers were attracted by promises of big state aid to set up in a particular country, even though the numbers did not make economic sense. Now they are wondering what plants to keep!! Consumers in the UK were disillusioned by what they saw as inflated car prices and began shopping around in Europe to import at keener prices, sometimes via the Internet. Sales had slowed in the USA and Europe (some 15%). Car manufacturing, especially in Europe in 2001, was predicted at 18m cars (Source: Commerzbank 2000) but predicted buyers were only 15m. Britain, outside of the Euro group, also faced higher exporting costs due to the strong pound. Manufacturers were having to shift production to newer, more efficient plants in Europe where several models could be made on one single production line. There was a strong suggestion that the new Vectra model, originally planned for Luton by General Motors, would now be made in Germany from 2003. Quite simply there was overcapacity in the industry and the "super" manufacturers like General Motors and Ford could not continue to carry the European losses any longer.

The new century was not looking good for Britain's car industry. Globalisation may have its advantages, but it comes at a price!

Note: *Information for this case has been collected from a variety of public sources. The figures have been adjusted to enable clearer relationships to be observed. The material is not intended to imply good or bad management practice. This mini case is presented as illustrative material and is suitable for teaching purposes only.*

PART A

Question 1.

a.   As a Marketing Consultant to a small volume (200,000 units per annum) car manufacturer of medium priced family cars which exports mainly to the UK (20% of production), write a report to the Chief Executive indicating the possible effects on the company of the shifts in global car manufacturing and marketing as described in the case. You may base the manufacturer in any country of your choice (except the UK).

(20 marks)

b.   The company is deciding to launch a new, highly fuel efficient, small car with every conceivable extra at a price slightly above similar, but much less well equipped, small cars. With a Marketing budget of $8m (or equivalent currency) for 2 years, devise an International Marketing Plan for 2002/3.

(20 marks)
(40 marks in total)

PART B – Answer THREE Questions Only

Question 2.

As a Marketing Consultant, advising a lesser developed country (LDC) provider of horticultural produce wishing to export to a developed country (DC), write a report showing the role of the international supply chain in creating value. Use "petrol" as an example for comparison.

(20 marks)

Question 3.

As a Marketing Analyst, write a report to an international manufacturer and marketer of cosmetics, on the use of Information Technology (IT), Information Systems (IS) and Information Management (IM) for evolving International Marketing Strategies.

(20 marks)

Question 4.

Choosing any international or global brand of your choice, write briefing notes for the Marketing Director on the role "culture" plays in global marketing planning.

(20 marks)

Question 5.

In International Services, "physical evidence", "people", and "process" are the major ways to evidence service benefits. As a Consultant to a global bank, suggest ways in which these elements can be used within the marketing mix to gain competitive advantage.

(20 marks)

Question 6.

As the company Marketing Executive, write a report to the Chief Executive of an international chemical company showing how following an environmentally friendly marketing strategy can lead to a better reputation.

(20 marks)

Question 7.

As a Marketing Consultant to an international organisation of your choice, show how the organisation can pursue marketing strategies which will add value for all its stakeholders.

(20 marks)

Appendix 4

- Are better structured and more logical.

- Use good examples.

- Apply underpinning theory, concepts and frameworks (there is no need to explain the theory or concepts); and

- Demonstrate an in-depth knowledge of international marketing, business, and management.

Part A

Question 1.

First of all you should get a feel for the firm in the Case Study for this paper and quickly identify some key issues. Although much of the material relates to the UK market, the firm – a small manufacturer of cars – is located outside the UK. You are able to choose the location of the firm.

20% of the production is mainly exported to the UK. The figures that are provided enable you estimate that, taking a typical average price of £10,000 and a production of 200,000 cars, the firm's annual turnover is £2bn, of which £400m comes from imports to the UK.

The examiner has asked you to take the role of a marketing consultant writing a report to the Chief Executive, who will expect the report to focus upon strategic issues and not get involved in operational detail. Your answers to parts a and b should be kept separate.

In your planning your answer you should identify some key themes which will act as subheadings for your report.

1a. This question is about the global macro environmental factors that are affecting the business. Your introduction should include two or three sentences that highlight the key issues. Although this is a relatively small company it is part of a global market and so its operations are affected by the changes in the global environment and moves in the car industry towards greater globalisation.

Changing environment and market structure

You should use a PEST plus market factor analysis (market structure, customers and competition) as a checklist to identify the most important factors and the effect that they are having on marketing strategies. Technology, increased competition and changing customer demands are clearly significant.

The structure of the industry is changing. There is over capacity and this is leading to consolidation and alliances amongst the car-makers as global companies become increasingly powerful and are able to locate major manufacturing facilities in any country of their choice (as against setting up a plant in every country). Technology (for example, e-commerce) is enabling new routes to market to be used, by-passing traditional routes that include dealerships.

The impact of the changes

As firms become more global and move their operations out of domestic economies then:

- Employment, income and skills can be lost.

- A range of stakeholders will be affected, including government, and consumers.

- Local suppliers are affected too, not only because of relocation of car manufacturers but also because component suppliers are also consolidating and becoming global players too, so there is the risk of takeover or much fiercer competition; and

- Supplying markets from outside the country can make it more difficult for the firm to see trends and plan effectively in that country.

Your conclusion should then briefly confirm the key points for the Case Study company.

1b. In the introduction to this question your selection of a country in which to locate the manufacturing capability is important. For example, subsidies are available for manufacturers in Korea and Malaysia. In developing a plan you should remember that the budget for marketing is small for a major global industry. The market overcapacity with too many suppliers means that competitors could respond aggressively to any aggressive strategy you might develop. The examiner would expect you to say whether you would concentrate on just the UK market or enter other markets too.

Your plan should take a conventional approach to presentation with sections on: analysis, marketing strategy, implementation, evaluation and control. Use a framework that you are familiar with to do this, for example, SOSTAC.

- **Analysis** of the environment, market and company capability using appropriate checklists or models, such as PEST and SWOT.

- **Strategy development.** You should consider identifying this in terms of the strategic focus (e.g. mass or niche market), segmentation, targeting and competitive positioning strategy and the market entry strategy.

- **Implementation plan.** This should include the 7Ps, 7S framework, timing, resource and budget priorities.

- **Control and evaluation**, including key areas for measurement and appropriate methods, such as benchmarking and balanced scorecard.

Part B (You are asked to choose 3 from 6 questions in this section)

Question 2.

This question is about the addition of value to basic commodities throughout the supply chain. Horticultural products are essentially raw materials that are transformed by the use of technology, production, people skills and marketing into products that are in a more useful form and more easily accessible. For horticultural products this would include cleaning them, trimming off leaves and roots of the plant, slicing or dicing, freezing, packaging them and distributing them through different types of outlets. As a result consumers are willing to pay more money for the products than they would be worth while still in the ground. By thinking in these terms you can see the comparison with 'petrol'.

Your answer should include a number of sections to address these issues.

An introduction might briefly explain the rationale for the question and the essential similarities between horticultural products and petrol.

The context

In answering this question you should again adopt the role of a marketing consultant advising the LDC provider of horticultural produce.

A key pointer in the question is the reference to an LDC, where you might expect limited resources, a weak domestic market (few consumers have the ability to pay for added value products) and a lack of marketing skills. Hence an export market needs to be found and a deal negotiated with members of the supply chain, and arrangements made for the processing and delivery of the products.

A section should highlight issues such as legislation covering imports of this nature, conditions of trade and the different requirements of the restaurant trade, supermarkets and small retailers.

Adding value through the supply chain

A section including an explanation of the supply chain and how value could be added at each stage (processing, packing, logistics, design of packaging, branding and negotiation of the role of the members of the supply chain) is necessary. Here it is important that the producer understands the export market requirements and remembers the effect of SRC in devising strategies.

Comparisons with petrol need to be made and examples provided to highlight some key issues, such as the relationship between LDCs and DCs, perhaps using Zimbabwe as a grower of high price horticultural produce and Shell sourcing oil in Nigeria.

Question 3.

Here it is important to answer the question that is asked, not to answer a question that you would like to have been asked – one which you had prepared an answer for during your revision!

This is not a general question requiring a discussion of information and its processing. It is specifically about how information can be used to support marketing strategy development by focusing upon the three elements. The examiner wants you to adopt the position of a marketing analyst writing a report to an international manufacturer of cosmetics. Your introduction should reflect these points.

The information process elements

By identifying the three elements in the question separately – IT, IS and IM – your first task should be to provide a definition or explanation of these terms and how they fit together in information processing. In doing this you are identifying the need for hardware, software and people skills to efficiently collect, store, and analyse data, and make decisions effectively. Take care to distinguish clearly between the terms and ensure that you use the terms in the appropriate context. Moreover, explain the challenges posed by applying these in an international market.

The main part of the answer should be to explain how IT, IS and IM can support each element of the planning process (analysis, strategy development, implementation, control and evaluation). For example, how they can be used to support the SLEPT analysis, decision-making and control and evaluation.

Explain how IT, IS and IM can work together to address the challenges that are posed in planning in international markets. Provide specific examples, for example, the use of databases, data mining, web enabled knowledge management, decision-making software.

Question 4.

This is a very straightforward question, but be careful with your first important task, which is to choose an international or global brand. Have pity on the poor examiner who gets bored reading about Coca-Cola and McDonald's! Because the question focuses on culture avoid products, such as computers, which may need to be adapted to different languages for the keyboard and instruction manual but which are not particularly culturally sensitive. These will give you little scope for examples in the industry sector.

Definitions

Taking a lead from the key phrases in the question, define or explain the relevant dimensions of an international or global brand, such as customer recognition, associations and perceptions of quality. You should also focus on the possibilities for standardisation and the need for adaptation.

Discuss the elements of culture taking care to go beyond those that are obvious, such as language and religion, and include values and attitudes, aesthetics, education, legal and political issues, technology, material culture and social organisations.

The role of culture

The main part of your answer should then focus on the role of culture in each element of the global marketing planning process (analysis, strategy development, implementation, evaluation and control). The examiner encourages you to consider the impact of culture on traditional planning concerns, for example, customer needs, product acceptance and promotional programmes, but also other areas, such as service expectations and customer relationship management.

Your examples will reinforce the points that you make. For a better answer, you should refer to the theories of writers, such as Lee (SRC), Hofstede and Hall, but don't discuss their work in detail; focus on its application.

Question 5.

Beware of questions like this where the unsuspecting candidate launches into a general discussion of services marketing and some associated theories without really reading the question!

You must adopt the role of consultant to a bank and demonstrate how these elements can be used to gain competitive advantage within that specific context.

The dimensions of international services marketing

Again being prompted by the question that has been set, it is necessary first to explain the dimensions of services marketing (especially how they differ from 'pure products') and the 3 additional service Ps.

This then leads to a discussion of the key challenges posed in internationalising services and using these elements to achieve success.

The People element should address not just the consistency of quality and responsiveness of the bank staff delivery, including those behind the counter and in call centres, but also the differing customer expectations of service from banks in different countries in the world.

The Physical Evidence would include the consistency of the corporate identity, the appearance of the branches, and the availability and use of new technology, such as Internet capability.

The Process would relate to how easy it is to access services from the bank, no matter where the customer is located, and how satisfied the customer is with the overall 'experience'.

Gaining competitive advantage internationally

The examiner has asked how these elements can be used to gain competitive advantage internationally. The challenge of physical evidence is to make tangible the intangible bank service, but the value of both tangibles and intangibles will be perceived differently around the world. In considering this, the following questions might be helpful:

Does the following create greater competitive advantage?

- A multinational or locally based corporate identity (Physical evidence).

- All or one of the following: having counter staff, telephone call centre or Internet banking (People).

- Speed of cheque clearance, funds transfers, accessibility to advice (Process).

You should then discuss the notion of competitive advantage and explain how it can be created on a global basis.

You should underpin your answer with relevant theory (including relationship management and service quality) and provide bank related examples.

Question 6.

Many students believe that a question like this requires specialist knowledge, or needs a lot of preparation, so they therefore avoid it. However, by using your general business and marketing knowledge, your experience and taking a professional approach, you should produce a good quality answer. A greater danger in this question is in not making your answer international. In adopting the position of Marketing Executive writing to the Chief Executive, the examiner is expecting you to provide an answer that addresses the benefits to the environment but also produces real benefits for the company.

In your introduction you should explain briefly that many of the company's stakeholders expect the company to adopt an ethical stance and develop and implement environmentally friendly policies, but their views might vary according to their cultural or country perspectives and priorities.

The key phrase in the question is 'lead to a better reputation'. You should explain that by effectively communicating the company's policies and actions to all stakeholders a positive reputation will be created and commercial stakeholders should be more willing to do business with the company. A negative reputation will lead major commercial stakeholders to question the company's standards and values and possibly mistrust the company.

Stakeholder expectations

Split the answer into sections. First, explain why environmentally friendly marketing strategies are important to stakeholders, such as governments, shareholders, customers, staff, employees and pressure groups.

Then address the role of the local country and international watchdogs such as Greenpeace, Friends of the Earth and consumer protection associations and explain how they exert pressure actively (for example, by directly targeting polluters with direct action and protests), and more 'passively' in helping to improve standards and values, by providing advice, running conferences and participation on policy committees. You might also mention the greater (although still limited) support for 'whistleblowers' (employees who report unacceptable company practices).

Bear in mind the international dimension. For example, the US and its companies pursue environmentally friendly policies selectively rather than comprehensively. It is also unacceptable for MNEs to pollute by exploiting weak environmental legislation in some LDCs. This may be legal but is unethical.

The implications of the environmentally friendly strategy

These should then be outlined. The marketing mix will provide a checklist. Some examples are:

- Manufacture and distribution – pollution reduction.
- Design and manufacture – recycling.
- Packaging – the use of recycled material.
- Labelling – explain the product issues and promote the company's stance.
- Promotion e.g. PR – to communicate standards and values to both the internal and external audience.
- Sponsorship – related international, national and local community activity.

The dangers of not adopting an environmentally friendly policy should be explained. Better global communication ensures that bad practice is more widely publicised and scrutinised. The company may be targeted as a polluter and its actions would be scrutinised more closely by the regulators and pressure groups. In extreme cases its business could be disrupted.

Higher marks in the question would come from international examples, explaining the difficult balance between commercial pressures and the need to be a good corporate citizen.

Question 7.

Questions 6. and 7. both focus on stakeholders. But when two questions on a paper appear to require similar answers, beware! You need to provide a much wider ranging answer and include a wider range of stakeholders. The international nature of your answer should be obvious.

Your introduction should briefly include:

- The concept of stakeholders.
- Their separate and often conflicting demands and expectations of the company.
- The need for managers to manage these different expectations of their stakeholders worldwide.

Stakeholders and their expectations

The stakeholders should then be identified and you should comment on:

- Their commercial, social, environmental, and community interests.

- Their domestic, host country or global perspective.

- Their power and influence over the company.

Marketing strategies relevant to the question

You should then identify some relevant marketing strategies in this context, for example:

- Market share growth.

- Harvesting.

- Market withdrawal.

- Cost reduction (e.g. by increased outsourcing at the expense of in-house production).

- Mergers and alliances.

And explain how these affect the different expectations of stakeholders, for example, in the domestic and host country.

Adding stakeholder value

The question focuses on adding value for all its stakeholders and you need to explain why and how stakeholders' value might be enhanced. In some instances this will require thought and you may even challenge this notion. For example, cost reduction may force the closure of an efficient factory in the domestic country and transfer of production to a low labour cost country (e.g. as has recently happened with Dyson vacuum cleaners), with an associated loss of jobs.

Better answers will provide good examples and explain the need to balance different expectations, as the above situation requires.

Appendix 5

Assessment guidance

There are two methods used for assessment of candidates – Examination or Continuous Assessment via project.

The Chartered Institute of Marketing has traditionally used professional, externally set examinations as the means of assessment for the Certificate, Advanced Certificate and Postgraduate Diploma in Marketing. In 1995, at the request of industry, students and tutors, it introduced a continuously assessed route to two modules, one at Certificate level, and one at Advanced Certificate. With the increased emphasis on marketing practice, all modules are now open to assessment through Examination or Assessed Project.

The information in this appendix will:

- Help you prepare for Continuous Assessment.

- Provide hints and tips to help you prepare for the Examination.

- Manage your time effectively in preparing for Assessment.

NB: Your tutor will inform you which method of assessment applies to your programme.

Preparing for continuous assessment

If being assessed by Project you will be given a full brief for the assignment which will include what you have to do, how it is to be presented and the weighting of marks for each section. **You must read this before you start and check your understanding with your tutor.**

The assignment will consist of a number of tasks with weighting, so make sure you take account of this in your final presentation of the project.

The size of the project will be identified by a recommended word count. Check your final word count carefully but remember that quality is more important than quantity.

The Assignment tasks will include a reflective statement. This requires you to identify what you have learned from the experience of undertaking the module and how you have applied that learning in your job.

Questions you might want to consider to help you write this reflective statement include: What was the most difficult part? How did you feel at the start of the exercise and how do you feel at the end? Did you achieve your objectives? If not, why not? What have you learned about yourself as you have worked through the module? How much of your learning have you been able to apply at work? Have you been able to solve any real work problems through work you have done in your Assignments?

This statement will be personal to you, and should look forward to points you have identified as needing work in the future. We never stop learning – keep up this process of Continuous Professional Development as you go through your studies and you will have acquired the habit by the time you need to employ it to achieve Chartered Marketer status!

Examinations

Each subject differs slightly from the others, and style of question will differ between module examinations. All are closed book examinations apart from Analysis and Decision (see below).

For all examinations, apart from Marketing in Practice (see below), the examination paper consists of two sections:

Part A – Mini-case, scenario or article.

This section has a mini-case, scenario or article with compulsory questions. You are required to make marketing or sales decisions based on the information provided. You will gain credit for the decisions and recommendations you make on the basis of the analysis itself. This is a compulsory section of the paper designed to evaluate practical marketing skills.

Part B – Examination questions.

You will have a choice from a number of questions; when answering, ensure that you understand the context of those that you select. Rough plans for each answer are recommended.

The examination for Marketing in Practice differs in that the compulsory questions and examination questions are all linked to the mini-case and additional relevant information given, such as memos and reports.

The examination for Analysis and Decision is an open book examination and in the form of a Case Study. This is mailed out 4 weeks before the examination and posted on the CIM web site at the same time. Analysis and preparation should be completed during these four weeks. The questions asked in the examination will require strategic marketing decisions and actions. The question paper will also include additional unseen information about the Case Study.

CIM code of conduct for examinations

If being assessed by this method you will receive examination entry details which include a leaflet entitled 'Rules for Examinations'. Read these carefully because you will be penalised by CIM if you are in breach of any of these.

Most are common sense. For example, for closed book examinations you are not allowed to take notes or scrap paper into the examination room and must use the examination paper supplied to make rough notes and plans for your answer.

If you are taking the Analysis and Decision examination ensure that you **do** take your notes in with you, together with a copy of the Case Study.

Hints and tips

There are a number of places that you will be able to access information to help you prepare for your examination if you are being assessed by this method. Your tutor will give you good advice, and exam hints and tips can also be found on the CIM web site.

Some fundamental points are listed below:

- Read the question carefully and think about what is being asked before tackling the answer. The examiners are looking for knowledge, application and context. Refer back to the question to help you put your answer in the appropriate context. Do not just regurgitate theory.

- Consider the presentation style of your answer. For example, if asked to write a report then use report format with number headings – not essay style.

- Structure – plan your answer to make it easy for the examiner to see the main points that you are making.

- Timing – spread your time in proportion to the marks allocated and ensure that all required questions are answered.

- Relevant examples – the examiners expect relevant theory to be illustrated by practical examples. These can be drawn from your own experience, reading of current journals and newspapers or observations. Visit 'Hot Topics' on the CIM web site to see discussion of topical marketing issues and practice.

Managing your time

What is effective time management?

It's using wisely one of your most precious resources – TIME – to achieve your key goals. You need to be aware of how you spend your time each day, and set priorities so you know what's important to you, and what isn't. You need to establish goals for your study, work and family life and plan how to meet those goals. Through developing these habits you will be better able to achieve the things that are important to you.

When study becomes one of your key goals you may find that, temporarily, something has to be sacrificed in favour of time needed for reading, writing notes, writing up Assignments, preparing for group assessment, etc. It will help to 'get people on your side'. Tell people that you are studying and ask for their support – these include direct family, close friends and colleagues at work.

Time can just slip through your fingers if you don't manage it – and that's wasteful! When you are trying to balance the needs of family, social life, working life and study there is a temptation to leave Assignments until the deadline is near. Don't give in to this temptation! Many students have been heard to complain about the heavy workload towards the end of the course, when, in fact, they have had several months to work on Assignments; they have created this heavy workload themselves.

By knowing how to manage your time wisely you can:

- Reduce pressure when you're faced with deadlines or a heavy schedule.

- Be more in control of your life by making better decisions about how to use your time.

- Feel better about yourself because you're using your full potential to achieve.

- Have more energy for things you want or need to accomplish.

- Succeed more easily because you'll know what you want to do and what you need to do to achieve it.

Finally

Remember to continue to apply your new skills within your job – study and learning that is not applied is wasted time, effort and money! Well done and keep it up.

Index

See also the Glossary on page 239.

You may find referring back to the Learning Outcomes and the Summary of Key Points at the beginning and end of each Session will aid effective use of the Index.

Only where subjects are relevantly discussed or defined are they indexed.